BREAKTHROUGH BOOKS

THE LION
IN THE
GATEWAY

938

The Last of the Wine
The King Must Die
The Bull from the Sea

A BREAKTHROUGH BOOK

THE LION IN THE GATEWAY

The heroic battles of the Greeks and Persians at Marathon, Salamis, and Thermopylae

by
MARY RENAULT

EDITED BY WALTER LORD

Pictures by C. Walter Hodges

HARPER & ROW, PUBLISHERS
New York, Evanston, and London

The translation of Æschylus' epitaph which appears in the Historical Note is reprinted by permission of The University of Chicago Press from THE COMPLETE GREEK TRAGEDIES, *edited by David Grene and Richmond Lattimore.*

CONTENTS

ILLUSTRATIONS

THE LION
IN THE
GATEWAY

I

THE ARROW
OF ORMUZ

Greece is a mountain land. In winter, snow falls on the heights; in spring, it melts and the streams flow roughly, washing the good earth down into the valleys and the plains. There, where the crops grow—olives and vines and barley—the people live. In ancient times, when people were fewer, each plain and valley was a kingdom, shut off by its hills from all the rest.

In the stony heights nobody lived but hunters, and outlawed robbers waiting in ambush for travelers crossing the passes, and the priests of the gods who loved high places for their sanctuaries: Apollo, Artemis the maiden huntress, or goat-legged Pan. But in summer, when the snow was gone and the yellow broom came out in flower, the boys went up there with the goats and sheep to get the summer grazing. They grew brave and hard, fighting off wolves and leopards from their fathers' flocks, out in all weathers, with no shelter but a mountain cave when a black storm broke and lightning cracked among the iron rocks, or in the night when the wolves' howl echoed like demons laughing. If they were afraid, they had only the gods to pray to: bright-haired Apollo with his bow and lyre, Zeus the Sky Father, or Pan who strikes men and herds with blind fear in lonely places but can be kind when he is a friend.

They needed all their courage when they were men. The food in the valleys was always short, they had to fight off raiders from their cattle, or pirates who came by sea; or sometimes their king would lead them out raiding themselves.

As the times grew less wild, they learned to live without robbery. When the people outgrew the food supplies, the king would say to his brother, perhaps, or his younger son, "It is time to found a colony."

The leader he chose would call to him the young ambitious men and people who were short of land to keep their children. They would get ready some ships, and put on them all their goods, and go coasting in search of good un-claimed land. The world was still half full, and often they found what they wanted empty, though sometimes they had to fight for it. When they got it, they would build themselves a village and a shrine for their guardian god whose image they had brought with them. They brought too some fire from the sacred hearth at home, keep-ing it tended all through the long sea voyage in a sheltered lamp. When they had settled in their new home, they kindled their own sacred hearth-fire from it. It showed their link with their mother city, which was as real to them as the bond of mother and child. Both sides acknowl-edged it; in war or danger they would always call on their first land for help.

As the bees swarm out from the hives when the young queens call them, these Greek adven-turers spread eastward, finding or taking land; there was no law between peoples then but the law of sword and spear. They went into the tall

hilly isles of the blue Ægean, where each island would be a kingdom of its own, which the founding prince would leave to his sons. Some sailed still farther, to the coast of Asia Minor with its deep bays and purple mountains. There with good harbors and good land they prospered; their villages turned to cities, their shrines to noble temples; but they never forgot their home lands, and the links still held.

Out of all these new kingdoms, some were sure to have bad kings. But these were not people to put up with oppression; making new countries out of nothing had made them independent and tough. They threw out, sooner or later, rulers that ill-used them, and sometimes decided to do without a king at all. In some states the chief men met to pass the laws, and this they called oligarchy, which means "rule of the few." Others called all the citizens together, and every man had a say in what was done, by vote or acclamation. These called themselves "people-ruled" cities, which is, in Greek, democracies. They would talk of their city rather than their country, though it meant the same. The world was full of dangers, from robbers or pirates or wild beasts or from the next-door neighbors. Men farmed the land, but seldom lived on it; they would ride back at sunset into the little town, and it was to that they felt they belonged. Many of these small city-states were only a few miles across; but some were growing fast.

They grew the fastest on the coast of Asia Minor, where Turkey is today. These lands they called Ionia, after Ion son of Apollo, from whom they claimed to be descended. It was a fine coast for shipping, full of harbors; the Greeks were good with their hands, skillful and inventive, and with their ships they traded what they made. The better their profit, the richer they could make their work; the craftsmen who had begun with bronze and stone could now use gold and marble; the women wove their robes with figured borders. Everyone had enough to eat and time to spare.

It was this free time they grew by. If they had spent it lying in the sun, or sitting waiting to be entertained, today they would be forgotten. But they loved life; they could not have enough of it. They listened to adventure tales, not to escape the dullness of their lives, but hoping their own deeds might be as famous. They were never bored. They liked to make things, and make them better each time. Above all, they wanted to know. They took nothing for granted; life's mysteries called them always further on. What is the universe made of? What shape is the earth? Does the sun really move around it? Where were our souls before we were born? When we speak of justice, exactly what do we mean? Some made such searches into truth their lifework; these were called lovers of wisdom, which is, in Greek, philosophers.

Others applied their knowledge; starting with mathematics, which cannot lie, they learned how to measure things too high or wide to reach; geometry, they called it. They could reckon the strength of buildings, and plot waterways through mountains in a true line. They watched diseases; through this the doctor replaced the sorcerer. From their beginnings we have gone on.

Where trade is good, so is travel; the Ionians got along the sea roads; and besides their vases and their bronzes and embroidered stuffs, they exported their ideas.

When their philosophers or their craftsmen reached a mainland city, they were thronged with eager learners; old men as well as young, for Greeks never let their minds get stiff. But there was no harbor where they stepped ashore so gladly as at Piræus, the port of Athens.

Athens was the greatest of their mother cities, renowned in their old songs. The poets called her violet-crowned, from the blue hills that ringed her plain: "Shining, violet-crowned, much sung; famous Athens, stronghold of the gods."

When the great invasion of the iron-speared Dorians came to end the Age of Bronze, Athens alone of the fortress cities had held out through the wars, and given refuge to fleeing men of many lands; princes and bards, goldsmiths and potters and vase-painters and sculptors had settled there to enrich her with their skills. Later, when the people outgrew the town and the farmlands, some had gone out to Ionia and the new colonies. When their descendants voyaged back and saw the rock of the Acropolis, with its temple of Athene, goddess of honored citadels, standing against the sky, they felt that their hearts and minds were coming home.

Pythagoras the philosopher came there, teaching the music of the spheres and the soul's reincarnation; there Sappho, the greatest poet of her day, sang love songs to the lyre. Athens was well repaid for showing courage and mercy in the cruel days when the old world died.

From the heights of the Acropolis one could look westward and see in the clear air of Greece, across the Saronic Gulf, the far tall mountains that hid the land of Sparta.

There lived the children of the fair-haired Dorians, the ancient foes, in the rich lands they had conquered. Centuries had passed since the great siege of Athens; broad lands and waters lay between them now, and they lived as fellow Greeks, for their races sprang of a common stock. Yet they had never grown together. At first, when the Spartans settled in to farm their subject fields, they had learned from the men they ruled, who, though they had no iron, had a good deal more civilization. For a time, beautiful things still came from Sparta. But later, for reasons that will be seen, they had stopped learning. Poets, vase-painters, and goldsmiths could make no living in Sparta, and philosophers who asked questions got short shrift. But, thought the Ionians, why go where no one wanted them, when Athens was friendly and near?

The Ionian cities grew, and the people with them. But meantime, in the high hinterlands, inland to the east, something was growing too. It was the empire of the Medes and Persians, where, as in Sparta, no one asked questions unless he was given leave. From the Scythian steppes to the Indus, from the Black Sea down to the Nile, stretched a vast unbroken web of despotic power.

The poor, hard-living mountaineers of Persia had bred a mighty conqueror, whose name was Cyrus. First he raised his tribesmen above the ruling caste of the Medes, till he controlled the empire. Then he took the great city of Babylon; it was his coming that Daniel read upon the wall at Belshazzar's feast. After Babylon, his eyes turned westward.

Meantime the Ionians, grown splendid in the arts of peace, were living at ease. They forgot the hard struggles of their forefathers' day in the mother cities; the frontier wars, when they scrambled over rough hills after stolen cattle, or beat pirates off while the women and children clambered panting to the hill fort. They forgot what it is to know, when one is hungry, cold, or tired to death, that one has got to go on whatever happens. They lived no longer with necessity. If they got tired of rowing, they would beach their ships and rest in the shade of the trees. Once they had competed in the wrestling schools to see who was the strongest, or in battle for the crown of valor; now they raced to be rich, to have the showiest house or the finest clothes and to be served by many slaves. So they were conquered easily by the neighbor King of Lydia, who was richer even than they. His name was Crœsus. He had gold beyond counting, as they counted then; he measured it by sacks and bushel baskets; he would have been many times a millionaire. He was generous, and made great presents to his friends and to the temples of the gods; he was also very vain, and liked his guests to call him the happiest of men.

One day he was entertaining Solon the philosopher, in his capital of Sardis, and thought he would like to hear it again from this wise and famous man; so he asked the leading question, "Who, do you think, is the happiest man you know of?"

Solon thought for a while, and answered, "A man called Tellus, an Athenian." Crœsus was surprised, for Athens was not a very wealthy city, and asked what Tellus had. "His city prospered in his lifetime," Solon answered. "He had good sons, who married well; and all his grandchildren lived to grow up. Then, when he was getting on in years, he fell in battle fighting gloriously, and his name is remembered with honor."

Crœsus was dashed by this reply, and could not keep from saying, "What about me?"

"Your life is not yet over," said Solon. "Do not tempt the gods by pride. When the sum of a man's finished days is known, then is the time to say if he was happy."

Time passed; and Crœsus, watching Cyrus' growing power, felt himself threatened, and resolved on war. Before he began, he sent to ask Apollo's oracle at Delphi what the outcome would be. The answer came back from the prophetess that if Crœsus went to war, he would

destroy a mighty empire. He was delighted, and
forgot to ask which empire it would be.

It turned out to be his own. The Persians
were hard mountain men, lean and sparely fed;
his troops were soft-footed and short-winded.
Crœsus was routed, his city sacked, and he himself trussed to a stake upon a pyre, to be burned
alive. Cyrus does not seem as a rule to have been
a cruel man; he worshiped a god of fire, and
perhaps meant Crœsus as a thank-offering for
victory. At all events, as they brought a faggot
to kindle the pyre, Crœsus cried out in his mis-
ery, "Oh, Solon! Solon! Solon!"

Cyrus heard him and wondered whom he
called on. Signing the executioners to wait, he
asked the doomed man who Solon was.

"Someone," said Crœsus, "whom every king
should talk to." And he told Cyrus the story. It
moved him so much that he had Crœsus taken
down and set on a seat beside him.

"You have shown me mercy," Crœsus said.
"May I tell you what is in my mind?"

"Yes," Cyrus answered, "speak out and do
not fear."

"Well, then," said Crœsus, "what is it your

troops are doing at present?"

"That is easy. Sacking your city and carrying off your wealth."

"Not mine," said Crœsus: "I have nothing any more. It is *your* wealth they are taking."

Cyrus was so struck with the good sense of this remark that, when he had stopped the looting, he took Crœsus into his household and kept him at court as long as he lived. But the cities of Ionia passed under the rule of the Medes and Persians, and were subject to their laws.

While Cyrus lived, they never tasted the bitter dregs of bondage; he was a great-hearted man and generous to the fallen. But when he died, the empire passed to his son, Cambyses, who was cruel, tyrannic, arrogant, suspicious and three parts mad. All the great powers Cyrus had had, but did not use unjustly, lay in the hands of this monster who could be called to account by no one. There was no law in the whole empire stronger than his fitful and savage whim.

He had a grave old courtier who had served his father and been much trusted. Cambyses too would urge him to speak frankly; but all he wanted to hear was flattery. One day the old man said to him, "Sire, since you asked for truth from me, I will tell you this from the good will I have to you: You should drink less wine. It is harming your health and your good name among the people."

At this Cambyses started up in rage. "Do you call me drunkard? I will show you whether my eye is straight. You, there, bring me my bow." When he had it, he aimed it straight across the banquet hall, where the courtier's young son was standing, and shot him dead. He had the body opened then and there, to prove that he had pierced the heart. And all the father dared do was praise his aim, knowing that if he showed grief or anger, he would suffer some dreadful death.

In time Cambyses died. He had murdered his own brother, and left no sons; so the crown passed to another line and a better man. Darius, the new King, though he had not Cyrus' greatness, was noble compared with Cambyses, and the Persians welcomed him thankfully. But the Greeks of Ionia had learned a lesson they would remember forevermore: that absolute power is no better than the worst man who can get it. In their hearts they knew they would not rest till they were free.

Meanwhile, in the Greek homeland beyond the islands and the blue Ægean, there had been wars and movement of peoples. In the little kingdoms between the mountain ranges, kings had come and gone, cities risen and fallen; and, here and there, dictators had appeared. There was one in Athens. After the passing of their kings they had been ruled by nobles, who looked out mainly for themselves; so Pisistratus, who was an able man, set himself up as the champion of the people. Though he tricked his way to power, when he had got it he was far from a bad ruler. He righted some of the people's wrongs, and took pride in the improvement of the city. One thing he did, for which the whole world is in his debt. Till then the poems of Homer had been passed from bard to bard, learned off by ear; in time they might have been garbled and half lost, or even have disappeared entirely. Pisistratus called the bards together, had their versions compared and the best ones chosen, and got it all written down. So we have the *Iliad* and the *Odyssey*, poems with so much life in them that every age has discovered in them something new. If he had never done another good thing in all his days, he would still deserve our gratitude.

However, he was a tyrant. We use the word now, rather vaguely, for a man who abuses power. In Greece it was just a term, like democracy, for a certain kind of government; it meant absolute rule by a man who had seized power, who was not a hereditary king. Pisistratus got his power with the consent of the Athenians; but once he had it, he never shared it; for better or worse, only his will was law. Athens put up with it: the nobles because they had to, and the people, on the whole, because they chose. But in due time Pisistratus died, and the power passed down to Hippias, his son.

A few years later, Darius, King of Persia, was sitting in his great hall, with his satraps and lords about him. Their long robes were rich with embroidery and golden fringes; their dark hair and beards were oiled, scented and combed. Sweet incense of burning gums rose up beside the columns of serpentine and polished basalt.

The wine was chilled with snow brought many miles from the mountains; and slaves waved great fans of peacock feathers set with jewels, to cool the air.

A chamberlain, whose duty was to greet guests and strangers, bowed to the King and said, "King of Kings, live forever. A Greek is here, not from these lands you rule, but from Greece beyond the sea. He says he is Hippias, an exiled ruler cast out by his subjects, and he begs your help."

"Exiled?" said Darius. "Why?"

"I suppose, Sire, he had too few spearmen. He is only a little king."

Darius nodded easily. "Is he hungry? Give him a place at table. He can make himself useful, somewhere about the court."

"My lord, he is asking for his throne again. If you will lend him troops, he says, to get his rights, he will make the Athenians your vassals, and do you homage for his kingdom."

"Who are these Athenians? I never heard of them. Some poor wild hill-tribe, I suppose, not worth a battle. Let him wait."

Darius turned back to his wine and the

princes round him. But presently there was a
stir by the doors. A royal courier had dis-
mounted, covered with dust and sweat. At
twenty halts, along the great royal road to Susa,
he had changed a worn-out horse for a fresh
one. He flung himself on his face before the
King, as the law required of him. Darius said,
"What news?"

"Great King, rebellion! The Ionians, un-
grateful for your gracious rule, sent to some
mainland Greeks, whom they say their fathers
sprang from, and begged their help. These people lent them ships and men. Sire, they have
burned the city of Sardis."

"Burned Sardis?" said Darius, staring.

"The thatch was fired, sire, in the battle when
they took the town, and the wind spread it. The
temple of Cybele the Great Mother lies in
ruins."

"All this," said Darius, "from the Ionians?
They gave no trouble before. Singers and danc-
ers, and talkers above all. 'What is the substance
of the universe? How heavy is the earth, and
why do not the stars fall down upon it?' Talk,
talk, talk; in the wine shops, in the streets, in

the gymnasiums. I have done as Cyrus did, given each city a Greek overlord, who owes his place to me and does as he is told. It served well enough, till now."

"It is these allies of theirs, Sire. The Ionians want to make their own laws and vote on them, as the Greek democracies do."

"Which Greeks do so? Their allies, you say?"

"Yes, King of Kings. It seems they had an overlord themselves, but cast him out. They say two young men rose up against him, because they had been dishonored by his house. The younger was killed in the first assault; the elder died under torture, because he would not name their comrades. The rising was quite put down. Yet soon after, the people rose again; other Greeks helped them; and Hippias lost his throne."

"Hippias?" said Darius. "I have heard that name before."

"Sire," said the chamberlain in his ear, "that is the exiled king, waiting outside. He ruled over the Athenians."

"The Athenians." Darius' lips moved in his dark beard; he was very angry. "I will remember these Athenians. And what is more, I will see that the gods remember."

He called his huntsman to bring him his great bow of horn bound with gold and silver, that he used when he stood in his two-horse chariot to shoot at lions. While the bow was coming, he ordered a scribe to write upon a strip of reed paper, "Mighty Ormuz, god of the noonday fire, grant me to be revenged on the Athenians."

When this message had been bound upon an arrow, Darius went into the courtyard. Bending the bow with all his strength (the Persians were great archers) he sent it speeding towards the sun. "So," he said, "Ormuz will remember. And I will remind myself as well." He called to him the slave who served him at table. "From this day forth, before food or drink shall pass my lips, say to me three times over, 'Sire, remember the Athenians.'"

The exiled tyrant, Hippias, stayed on as Darius' guest, planning with him how to betray his city; he would rather rule Athens as a Persian vassal than not at all. But all this while the Ionian Greeks, whom the Athenian fleet had

helped to conquer Sardis, grew bold with their success, and dreamed of throwing off their chains forever. They forgot, however, the old Greek saying, that he who wills the end must will the means.

One summer day, a Greek ship was sailing to the coast of Sicily, when the captain saw a pirate giving chase. Those seas were full of them. She was a fast penteconter, a galley of fifty oars. He shouted to the rowing master to make the rowers double their pace. "Use the whip if you must. They'll be thrown to the sharks if the pirate catches us."

The men rowed till they were nearly dropping at the oars, not needing the whip, for they knew what pirates did; but the galley took the wind of them, and the captain, seeing all was lost, said, "Let them rest." He waited on his poop, wondering if the pirate would sell him into slavery, hold him for ransom, or murder him out of hand.

But when the pirate captain came on board, he said, "I'm sorry, Captain, to wear out your rowers for you. You were sailing into the sun, or

I'd have seen you were from Athens. I do no business with Greeks."

The Athenian captain knew him then, and cried, "By Poseidon! You're Dionysos of Phocæa."

The pirate was a brown tough man, with a face that had been cheerful and open, but now was growing hard. "The same," he said. "Living as best a seaman can who's lost his city. Are you surprised to see me privateering, me who had my own squadron not long since?"

"No," the Athenian said, for now he understood.

He opened a jar of wine in his little cabin, and Dionysos said, "What news of the war?"

"Miletos has fallen," said the Athenian. "Lesbos will have gone by now. I wish I'd better news for you. Well, you did what one man could."

"You may say so," the pirate answered. "Yes; that you can say. When the Ionian cities first revolted, the spirit was good enough. Darius sent envoys to each town to threaten us, and each town sent them packing. We gathered the fleet at Ladé; and a good show it made. I brought my own three triremes, and we settled down to war maneuvers: rowing in line, javelin throwing, coming in to ram, and all the rest. The first day went well. The second day, my ships were the only ones that turned out. The rest of the fleet was beached, with the crews ashore all lying in the shade."

The captain nodded; he knew the customs of Ionia. He said, "They've not had to live as hard as we in Attica."

"And so I told them. I stood up in Assembly, and spoke my mind. 'We're on the edge of a knife,' I said, 'between being free men or slaves. And slaves caught on the run; remember that. Isn't it worth a little sweat, to save your cities? Let me take over the battle drill, and I'll make this fleet fit to go to sea."

The Athenian captain smiled grimly. "How long did it last?"

"A week, by Zeus! A week. Every day I took them out. I put them through the least a ship needs to come out of a sea fight floating: no more than that; I could see how soft they were. They want their fathers' freedom back; but they've forgotten how their fathers kept it. 'The lads at

Athens,' I said to them, 'train harder for a row-ing match than you're training for war. I want watches set tonight, not all sleeping ashore; and now, if you please, we'll try rowing abreast.' And then it came. 'What have we done,' they started shouting, 'to bring down the wrath of the gods on us like this? He talks of slavery! What does he give us now, the loud-mouthed bully? We're sick,' they said. 'This life will be the death of us. And who is he, to run us ragged like this? He only brought three ships of his own along.' Well, that was the end. They beached, and made camp like a lot of soldiers. When the Persians came, it was like hawks against day-old chicks. I'm one of the few that got away—with a price on my head, to live off Carthaginian merchantmen."

He went on to tell a tale of burned cities and slaughtered men, of women and children carried away to slavery. He ended, "Cherish your free-dom, you Athenians. Sell it dearer than you bought it first. Before, you were only subjects of a tyrant; but if the Persians bring Hippias back, you'll be the slaves of a slave."

But there was rejoicing in the lofty halls of Susa, where King Darius held his victory feast.

The wine went round in gold and silver cups from the sacked temples, which had once poured offerings to the gods. Greek slave boys served it; between the courses there was dancing by Greek slave girls, who dared not weep. But before the first mouthful of the banquet touched the lips of the King, the servant by him, who never forgot his orders, whispered in his ear, "Sire! Remember the Athenians!"

"Yes," said Darius. "Yes; it is time."

And he sent word to his cities to make ready his ships for war.

II

EARTH AND WATER

The business of preparing a great campaign got under way. It would be folly, Darius thought, while he was conquering Athens, not to subdue the rest of Greece as well. His armies would then have a clear passage; and his empire would be greater still. Indeed, since Rome was not yet important, he would be ruler over almost the whole known world.

So he sent his heralds across the Hellespont, some to each city-state and country, to make this proclamation: "Your lord, Darius, King of Kings, asks you for a token of earth and water, in sign of your land's homage. If you accept, and give his troops assistance when they pass through, you will be under his protection. If you refuse, he will treat you as his enemies."

The heralds were variously received. The Scythians of Crimea took little notice. Darius had tried before to subdue these restless neighbors. But wherever he had heard they were, when he got there they had gone; as was natural, since they were nomads seeking pasture. At last he lost patience, and sent a herald to say, "Why do you keep running away from me? Either fight me or do me homage. You must come to one or the other in the end." The Scythian king sent a message back; "What do you mean? We are not running from anyone, but living our usual lives. What should we fight you for? We have no cities; everything we own is in our wagons and we take it with us. Just keep away from our fathers' burial ground; if you meddle with that you will be sorry. As for your calling yourself my lord, you can run away and cry." So this time, Darius left the Scythians alone.

In Athens and in Sparta, the people were so enraged that they forgot all law and decency and killed the heralds, though all such messengers were sacred to the gods. They repented this deed in shame and fear, acknowledging their sacrilege. The Spartans began at once to get unlucky omens. They feared the gods would punish them with plague or earthquake; so, as they had killed two heralds, they called for two volunteers to give their lives for Sparta, and go to Darius offering blood for blood.

Two men came forward, Sperthias and Bulis, from the noblest families in the kingdom. Their courage was the more, because they knew the Persians practiced torture on those whom they put to death. But to save their people, they set out on the long journey over the sea and through Ionia, inland to Susa.

On their way they were brought before Hydarnes, the Satrap of Ionia and Commander of the Royal Guard. A good soldier himself, he admired and pitied them, and offered them supper at his splendid house. When the rich feast was over, he said, "You are being foolish. You need not die. The King honors brave men as I do. If you submit, he will take you into his service. Look at this house of mine; look at this table; look at the gold I wear. See how King

Darius rewards his faithful servants."

The Spartans answered, "Yes, Hydarnes. But you know only half the story. You who have never tasted freedom, how can you tell if it is sweet? If you had known it, you would be saying to us now, 'Defend it to the last.' "

So they went on their way to Susa, and were led into the presence of the King. But when they were ordered to prostrate themselves before him, as the custom was, they said, "Never! You can do no worse than kill us; we have come for that. Why should we disgrace Sparta as well?"

Darius signed to the guards to let them go, and answered like a king. "I will not do as your people did, and break the sacred law of nations; nor, after having denounced their crime, will I stoop to it myself. Let them bear their curse; why should I take it off them by killing you? Go back and tell them so; I give you my safe-conduct."

So these brave men went home; and after their offer of their lives, the evil omens ceased.

To the kingdom of Macedon, in the north, Darius sent no heralds, but a royal embassy. It was the biggest state upon his land route; a mountainous border country of fierce warriors, proud and revengeful, perhaps not much unlike the Afghan hillmen of later days. The southern lands only half counted them as Greeks; but the royal house had Greek blood, and valued it. Darius wished to impress these people with a show of power. Instead of heralds, he sent seven Persian lords, riding in carriages of state, with a suite of attendants.

Amyntas, King of Macedon, was old and ailing. He was cowed, as he was meant to be. He pictured his people slaughtered or sold as slaves, and gave the earth and water of submission, which made him henceforth a subject king. The rite of humiliation was performed; the Persians smiled. But there was one who did not smile; the king's young son, Alexander, looked on in anger and bitter shame. He felt himself a Greek; he had run at Olympia, where foreigners were barred, and tied to win. But he belonged too to Macedon, and its fierceness was in his bones.

He was young; the Persians thought nothing of him. Easy success had made them proud and insolent.

That night Amyntas ordered them a royal

feast. He hoped they would praise him to Darius, so that his troops would spare the land. The tables shone with gold and silver, and creaked under food and wine. Macedonians were known for their hard drinking; but the Persian envoys surpassed them all. As they drank, their fine manners slipped away. They felt like conquerors, and showed it. Presently they asked the King to send for the royal ladies, to share the feast.

This, anywhere in Greece, was a deadly insult. Greek ladies never mixed with strangers, with men especially; they met only relatives and old family friends. To bring them here would be treating them like paid entertainers, dancing girls, or slaves; only such women ever appeared at drinking parties. But in his fear, the poor old king consented.

Unwillingly, their veils drawn over their faces, the ladies came into the banquet hall, and sat shyly down on seats against the wall, as far as possible from these unknown men.

The young prince watched in rage. He would soon, as he guessed, be king; he felt his own honor dragged in the dirt by this servility. In-

sults were not borne well in the royal house of
Macedon. A few generations later, another of
their Alexanders would begin with Persia on
his way to conquer the world.

Presently the Persian envoys whispered to
each other, "The old man is frightened; we can
do better yet." One said aloud, "Surely, my
Macedonian friend, it would be better for these
ladies not to have come at all than treat us with
such coldness. Do ask them to sit beside us. After
all, you have given earth and water to our
King."

Too much ashamed to meet their eyes, Amyntas asked them to go over. The Persians, now
very drunk, started at once to kiss them. Amyntas felt a touch upon his arm. His son stood by
him, white with anger. "Father," he said, "you
look tired. You had better rest. Do not sit out
the drinking. Leave these people to me; I will
see they are taken care of."

The old man, sick indeed with shame, longed
to be gone, but his mind misgave him. "Why,"
he said, "do you want me out of the way? In the
gods' name commit no folly, or you will be the
ruin of us all. You are young; you do not know

the miseries of the conquered. Endure what
they do in silence. Then I will go. Indeed I can
bear no more."

No sooner was he gone than Alexander
turned to the envoys. He was now quite calm;
he even smiled. "Most honored guests, we are
happy that these ladies, our mothers and our
sisters, find favor in your eyes. But they came in
haste, just as they were; they would be sorry
not to look their best. Let them change and
adorn themselves, while you drink another
round. You will be able to say, I think, that here
in Macedon you were treated as you deserve."

Bemused with wine, the Persians never saw
him slip out after the women. "Quickly!" he
said. "Each of you give me her best robe and
veil. Then lock your doors." When they were
gone, he called for the Companions, his personal
guard of youths about his age; he picked out
seven, the youngest, with fresh smooth faces,
and gave them their instructions.

Soon after, there slipped into the supper room
seven graceful figures in rich robes, modestly
veiled. The Persians hailed them rowdily, and
made room on the seats beside them. But as they

reached to snatch the veils away, each found a strong hand at his throat, and a dagger plunged in his side. So they died, on the embroidered supper couches, among the gold and silver drinking cups, the young men stifling their cries. Alexander said grimly, as they were dragged away to their secret midnight burial, "You came for earth and water. Be content with earth!"

The embassy to Macedon vanished from the face of men, and King Darius awaited its return in vain.

But from many lands of Greece the heralds came back satisfied, with tokens of earth and water. Some gave from faintness of heart, or because they had little choice, being small and weak or badly placed for defense; some had self-seeking overlords like Hippias, who would keep their own wealth no matter how. But some cities chose to "Medize" (as other Greeks called it in contempt) because neighbors they were at feud with had defied the Persians, and they saw a chance of revenge. Blood-feud; revenge; they were the curses of the ancient world. They took no account of innocence; children, kinsmen, fellow clansmen, even babes in arms, might be

butchered with the man who had done the wrong. Only the Jews had the moral justice to put a limit on vengeance, "An eye for an eye, a tooth for a tooth"; no more. Elsewhere, a man thought little of himself if he only got his own back; he expected to go one better. In Persia, revenge was even crueler than in Greece; but the Greeks could harm themselves with it more, because they were more free. Darius knew it; he had counted on these old grudges between little nations. It was only after their ordeal still to come that the Greeks began to feel how much they had in common.

In rocky, sea-bound Attica, the country of Athens, the war-rumors were coming in from here and there. Before long they knew the worst; a ship came from the Ægean with the news that a great Persian war fleet was coming straight towards them, taking the quickest route through the islands of the Cyclades. Darius still remembered the Athenians.

The central island of the Cyclades is Delos. Though small and barren, it was one of the holiest places in Greece; it had risen from the sea, the legends said, to be Apollo's birthplace.

Like a shrine or temple, it had no defenses. At the sight of the Persian fleet, the priests and people fled to the nearest island, leaving it quite empty.

The Persians came. They stepped ashore upon the glittering rocks, pale gray, sparkling with silvery mica under a fierce, beating sun. There was no sound, no voice; only a lake with four stone lions watching it, and the tall straight image of the archer god, splendid and young, staring with still, secret eyes into the dazzling sky. Suddenly they were afraid, and offered a load of incense on his altar, and went away. But it would not be long before they got to Attica.

"Well," said the Athenians, "they must pass Euboea first." This was a long offshore island. "We sent the Euboeans troops to guard their coasts, and their own are good." But the men from Delos answered, "Your troops are coming home; we met them. The Euboeans will not stand; since Ionia fell, the very name of Persia makes men tremble. Some have fled into the mountains; some will surrender. They begged your men not to await destruction but fight for their own homes."

So the leaders of Athens, the archons, met the generals in council, and all agreed: "If Eubœa will not fight, we have only one hope left. We must send word to Sparta."

Now indeed it was time to remember the fair-haired Dorians of the south.

Philosophers did not visit them, nor bards, nor carvers of gems. They were ignorant, or forgetful, of all the arts save one; but that they worked at from the cradle to the grave. The art of Sparta was war.

The land they took in old days with their iron spears had been famous for many centuries; Helen the Beautiful met Paris there, and fled with him to Troy. But the Dorians were harder and stronger, as iron is harder than bronze. They burned the rich cities, killed the kings and warriors; but the people they kept as slaves. Slaves were the wealth of the ancient world; their labor set their masters free for hunting and fighting and the pleasures of life. So the race of the Helots still survived, but to a life of serfdom, tilling the fields of their Spartan lords and herding their cattle.

There is an ancient proverb, " 'Take what you

want and pay for it,' says God." The Spartans took, and paid. They were tough and brave, but few. The Helots, though brought so low, were many. As years and centuries passed, fear of a Helot rising governed the Spartans' lives from birth till death. Almost as soon as they could walk, they started to train for battle, living rough and sleeping hard; never allowed to cry if they were hungry, cold or in pain—which was often, for they wore only one thin tunic summer or winter; were kept short of food so that they would learn to live off the land; and, in their boyhood, were taken to the temple once a year and beaten till they bled, to try how well they bore it. Only strong boys survived to manhood; and if a baby looked sickly, they did not wait to see, but killed it when it was born. They had no time left for making music or the fine Laconian jars that once had been their pride; they ceased to question what men should be, or why, or how the world is made. They were at the other end of life from the Ionians.

Their boast was to be masters of the Helots, but to call no man master themselves. Though they still had kings, they had two at a time;

descendants of twin brothers, it was said; and the power of the kings was strictly watched. In peacetime, they had to obey the Council of the Ephors; it was only when he led his troops to battle that a Spartan king's word was law. To the needs of war, everything else gave way. If a mother saw her son carried back dead on his shield by his comrades, she only asked if he had fallen bravely. If he had, it was thought a disgrace to weep.

So when the Athenians heard that the Persian host was near, they said, "The Spartans will never endure a foreign yoke. If we send them word, they will march to help us."

At first they meant to send a ship, which was the quickest way; but the winds were contrary; and a horse would have been useless, for no one yet had thought of shoeing horses, and it would have been lamed on the stony mountain roads. They said, "We must send a runner."

They went, therefore, to the chief gymnasium of Athens, where the athletes, stripped and rubbed down with oil, were at exercise, or training for the Games: wrestling, or throwing the javelin at the mark, or scuffling in the pancration, which was an all-in of wrestling and boxing mixed. The runners were practicing the long jump, with stone weights in their hands to swing them farther—light lean young men, moving gracefully. The Greeks thought there was something wrong with any sport which did not make a man's whole body balanced and beautiful, as well as strong and quick. The Games were sacred to the gods, who asked perfection. While the young men jumped, a musician played on a flute, to give them rhythm.

The archons said to the trainer, "Who is the best of all your runners?"

He answered at once, "Pheidippides. At the All-Athenian Games in Athens he won the victor's wreath, and at the Isthmian Games at Corinth; he was crowned too at Delphi, though men from the coast can seldom win in that mountain air. Now he is in training for Olympia itself, and I think he will bring back the olive garland, the crown of crowns."

The archons said, "May it be so; but that is for another day. You say he can run in the mountains? Good; bring him here."

The trainer called. A young man left the line,

and stood respectfully before them. Pheidippides, in Greek, means "shining horse," and it
suited him well. He was slim and limber, hard
muscles moving sleekly under a skin polished
like silk with the oil of the gymnasium. He
looked swift, faithful and brave.

They told him his mission, and how much
would hang on it. Then they gave him the
written message, and taught him a speech as
well, for there were many Spartans who could
not read; when the war drills were finished, the
boys were too tired to learn. He took a little
bag of coin, which weighs lighter than food to
carry, and a cloak of light wool for the cold
nights in the mountains; and started on his way.
Already, when he left, Euboea had been taken.
From the coasts of Attica they could look across
the narrow strait at beaches black with Persian
ships.

He did not see them; his road lay westward.
First came the low green hills of Daphne, with
Apollo's laurel grove and shrine; then the road
ran beside the water of the Straits of Salamis,
through the plain of Eleusis. He saw, as he ran,
the temple of Demeter the Mother, where he

had been initiated into the Mysteries while he was still a boy. He remembered the wait in frightening darkness, then the great light, the singing, and the glorious sight that one must swear never to tell of, but which made one better forevermore. "Holy Mother," he prayed, "Giver of perfect gifts, bless us now, and in our death-hour when we cross the River. I have drunk your mixed drink; I have carried my torch to the sea-shore . . ." Then he fell silent, lest even in solitude he might break his oath.

He passed the harbor, with the ships making for Salamis; but still the wind blew contrary, and he knew now he must run the whole of the way.

After he had passed through Megara, he came to the Isthmus, the narrow neck between the mainland and the Peloponnese. Here in old days the hero Theseus had cleared the road from robbers and monsters who preyed upon its travelers, had wrestled with the murderer Sciron and thrown him off the cliff. The pale dusty track threaded the hillsides, and down below was the sea, deep blue and green, washing the feet of the dark crags. He longed to plunge down into it, to cool himself and sluice away the hot dust of the road. But he had measured his time, so much for food and rest, an hour or two for sleep, the least he could do with to keep going.

He sighted Corinth, the round-topped mountain wreathed with walls, and Isthmia where they held the Games of Poseidon, lord of the earthquake and the sea. There in the stadium he had waited at the starting stone, his toes against the grooves, while the umpire called out, "Runners! Feet to the line!" He remembered the last lap, only the man from Sparta still in front; the gathering of his strength for the final sprint. But he was running now against unseen antagonists—time and fate.

Resting a little, and drinking from the streams, and eating sparely, he ran on and on, in high, hot noon and in the sunset and under the rising moon and in the gray of daybreak: up into the hills of Argolis, past the squat stone keep of Mycenæ, brooding on its ruined greatness and its ancient curse; then up and up, into the great range of Taygetus that bounds Sparta to the north. "The hardest lap," he thought, "will be coming last."

He was up in the thin cold air, higher than the pure blue air of Delphi where he had been crowned in Apollo's temple on the mountainside. Here all was bare rock, and watercourses scoured as clean as bone; harsh thorn bushes and sparse scrub, a bare living for goats; around and above, more peaks, blue in the distance, veined in their cracks and gullies with frozen snow.

He had run at Delphi fresh; now he was weary; his chest was laboring, for every step he needed a new breath, the cold air seemed to stab his lungs like a sword. And he thought, "I shall never run now at Olympia. This day has broken my strength; I feel a flaw in the iron, a crack in the jar, that won't be mended. They will never carve my name in marble, to be remembered forever; never the wreath of wild olive, the crown of crowns . . . But, if the Persians win, no more Olympia at all, no honor, no sacred games. Better than winning, to give them back to Hellas for evermore."

He labored on through the passes, skirting the edges of great black ravines, knowing one false step could send him down where only the wolves would find him; then out into the teeth of the wind. His heart was pounding when he stopped to rest, and he thought, "I shall die if I go on. I cannot do it." Then he thought of his city burned and sacked; his mother and little brothers carried away to slavery, and the girl he was in love with, dragged shrieking to the Persian ships. He had held nothing back; he was ready to die with that day's sunset if he could give his message first; but if he died here on the wild mountain, who would be the better for him but the vultures and the wolves? There was nothing to do but pray. He was far from the gods of home; but as he stumbled on, he panted out a prayer to whatever god might hear him.

When he opened his eyes, the dark mountains still swam around him. But his loneliness had left him, and the fear of the empty places; it seemed to him now that the wilderness had become his friend, and he was alone no longer.

Someone was keeping pace with him, breathing like a runner with strength to spare; he heard the steady rhythm, yet there was no thud of feet, only the click of trotting hoofs. His sight was dimmed with blackouts coming and going; but when it cleared he saw beside him horns, a

long goat beard, and strange yellow eyes. And
he thought, in the dream of his great weariness,
"It is Pan, driver of herds, lord of the waste-
lands; the god of the place, to whom I prayed."

He uttered in his dream some salutation; his
lips did not move, he was running with all his
breath; and it seemed that Pan replied to him,
mixed with a wild music like a reed pipe in the
wind, "You all forgot me in the city; yet I am
here." The echoes came back from the iron rocks
and gullies. "I am here . . . I am here . . . !"

The shaggy god was close to him, he caught
the rank, strong goat smell, and heard the kicked
pebbles fly. "I am your friend, Pheidippides,
Shining Horse of Athens. I was honored once in
Attica, before men lived in cities. Why do they
forget?"

So he ran in a kindly dream, with Pan beside
him, who could stampede great herds of cattle
with a breaking twig, or send a man in headlong
flight, without reason, through a lonely wood,
so that he would say later, "Why did I run? It
was panic, the madness of the god." But he felt
no fear, only a comfort, as if some great friendly
beast had come to keep him company. At last

he came into the foothills, where the going was downhill and the air was stronger. His head and his eyes grew clear, and he found himself alone. No living creature was in sight, save a wild he-goat standing on a crag; but he knew he could get to Sparta now, before his strength gave out.

At last he came to the city of thatched huts beside the broad stream of Eurotas (the Spartans had no time to spare for carving marble) and the people crowded round him to hear the news. When they learned that in two days he had run a hundred and fifty miles, they said, "Not bad." It was a point of pride with the Spartans to waste no words.

After he had rested for a while, and drunk some wine, he came before the Council of the Ephors. When they had heard his message, they all agreed that the Persians must not rule in Hellas; that troops should be sent to Attica to man the coast. "But," they said, "it is the moon's first half, and we start no new business before full moon. That is our ancient law."

"But," said Pheidippides, who could scarcely believe his ears, "that is not for five days! Marching with heavy arms, it will take you five more to get there. And the Persians, if they cross the straits to Marathon, can be at Athens in a day."

"That is with the gods," said the eldest ephor. "Here in Sparta, the customs are never changed."

Pheidippides went to his bed of rushes in the guest hut, heavy of heart. Though the bed was rough, he was tired enough to have slept on marble. He thought, before he closed his eyes, "In Athens, when we were ruled by Hippias, we called it tyranny. It seems there is another kind that men make in their own souls. As boys they must question nothing; as youths they must think alike, what they are told. And when they are men, there is a fetter of iron around their minds."

Next day he went down to the coast, for the wind that had stopped his sailing there would blow him home. He thought of Pan, and the struggle that had almost killed him, and how he would never run, now, at Olympia with his strained heart. It would have been all the same, he thought, if he had taken it easy, bathing in the cool rock pools, resting in the heat of noon, saving his strength for Olympia and the glorious olive crown. And indeed his name was never carved in marble and put up in the temple of Olympian Zeus. But the temple has fallen, the carved names have been gone a thousand years; while famous Herodotus, who wrote the history of the war, put in the story of his run, and how he met Pan in the mountains. Because of him and the battle he brought warning of, a long cross-country run is still called a Marathon; and his name has come down with honor to our own day.

III

TRUMPETS
AT MARATHON

Meantime, in Athens, all able-bodied men and youths had armed themselves, and prepared for war.

They marched across Attica, from the western to the eastern seaboard; over the passes of Hymettus, and down through the olive groves, till they saw below them the wide blue Bay of Marathon, with its crescent plain and its beaches of drifted sea wrack. Already the Persian ships were beached there, so many that they almost hid the shore. They saw the tall galley of the general, Datis, with a high chair on it from which he could watch the fleet, and the Persian bowmen shooting at sea gulls, to keep in trim.

The Persians took their time, having many men to organize; and the Athenians waited too, for they saw they were outnumbered ten to one, and they thought the Spartans were on the way. As they waited, they thought how Theseus the hero-king had tamed the wild bull there, which was laying waste the land; for him it had been a lucky battleground, and it gave them hope.

Then they heard the news that their runner brought from Sparta, and knew that they stood alone.

There on the foothills, looking down on the teeming beaches, the Athenians held a war council.

There were no regular armies in Greek cities then, except where some tyrant kept his guards; and of these the people had a horror, once they had got their freedom. The troops were all free citizens, called out where there was need; and, lest one man should seize power again, they had not even a supreme commander. The chief generals took turns to lead. This was, of course, democracy run mad. It would not have stood the test of a major war; but it did not need to, for that day's turn had fallen to a wise and decent man. Instead of clinging to his office in the hope of a victor's fame, he offered it at once to the most experienced officer, whom everyone had faith in. Miltiades was his name. The general who stepped down was called Aristides. This was only one of many times he had put the people's good before his own; because of this, the Athenians called him Aristides the Just.

Now they had a leader, but still no plan. The swarms on the shore appalled them. Some of the officers, good fighting men or they would not have been promoted, said it might be better to ask for terms, and even take Hippias back again, rather than give up the city to Ionia's fate. They retold the dreadful stories, already too well known.

"Stop!" said Miltiades. His courage had risen while theirs was wavering. They fell silent, and gave him hearing.

"We have still a chance," he said, "if we strike today, while our hearts are good, before the Persians guess our allies have failed us. From here you can see only the numbers of the enemy; but take my word for it, their skins are soft. Look at them, covered with clothes all over, even their legs and arms. Who ever saw a Persian naked to sun and wind, upon the wrestling ground or the race track? Strip one, and you'll find him white as a slug. They are even ashamed to have their bodies seen, sure sign of a barbarian. I am for war; but I'm no tyrant, to force you into it. You have the right to vote."

Five voted with him; five more against; and there was one vote to come, that of the War Archon, whom we might call the Secretary of Defense. Miltiades turned to him. "Well, Callimachus? Everything rests with you. Will you bring Athens down to slavery, or point her to freedom and eternal fame? If we bow to the Medes, we know what miseries await us. If we fight and win, we shall be the glory of Greece and her greatest city. It rests with you alone."

There was a pause of destiny. Then Callimachus said, "I vote to attack."

"You have earned the post of honor," said Miltiades, and put him in command of the right wing. The right was the spear side, the left the side of the shield.

Then the priests sacrificed, and found the

omens good. Miltiades looked at the men before him, drawn up in tribes; those from each village and district grouped together, knowing each other and full of family pride. He saw them keyed up with desperate courage; now or never! He shouted "Charge!" and led them downhill at a run.

Nearer they came. The crowds of Persians seemed to be doing nothing. In fact, the sight had stunned them; this handful of madmen, running to their doom as if for sport. Then came the shrill Greek battle yell, calling the war god: *"Allala Ares! Allala Ares!"* nearer and nearer, like the cry of the swooping eagle. It roused the Persians, and the archers drew their bows. But it was hard to hit running men holding their shields above them; the arrows bounced off like rain, and the men of Athens felt uplifted by their speed, as if some great wind bore them on.

Greek soldiers carried two spears each, one to fight with and one to throw. As they neared the Persian lines, they hurled their javelins. In the thick ranks that had looked unbreakable, men fell and gaps appeared. The Greeks dashed onward; the hosts met hand to hand. Now it was

close shield and spear work, thrusting and stab-
bing, face to face and knee to knee.

So long was the Persian battle line, so short the
Greek, that Miltiades had feared the wings
would be outflanked, and had massed his men
there, leaving the center thin. The left wing was
held not by Athenians, but by men from Platæa.

It was a town to the north of Attica; a small
place, whose men were brave but few. Years ago,
being beset with enemies, they had sent to
Sparta, offering the Spartans a pact of mutual
aid. But the Spartans did not care for allies so
far away; what if, while they were off helping
the Platæans, their own Helots rose? "Apply to
Athens," they said, "which is nearer, and can
come quicker to your help." Let the Athenians,
they thought, take on the Platæans' quarrels, and
if it got them into trouble, so much the better.
Athens was getting more powerful than Sparta
liked.

The Platæans took them at their word, and
went to Athens. And the ancient stronghold,
which had sheltered so many hard-pressed
people in the old wars, made them welcome and
pledged a vow of friendship. At the time of need,

the Athenians fought their enemies and made their boundaries secure. Never was help more generously repaid.

For now, when the hordes of Persia bore down upon the Greeks, the deep wings held, but the center started to give. The men there fought like heroes; but sheer weight was crushing them. It seemed they might be cut in two, and everything would be over.

The sheltering hills were near; Hymettus could have hidden a thousand men. The Platæans might have thrown down their heavy shields, run for their lives, and made for home. But they had pride and honor. Athens had defended them; now was their time to pay the debt. With a mighty heave they broke the Persian line before them; the enemy scattered toward the ships, dropping in their flight choice weapons and handsome shields, a rich prize for the taking. But the Platæans let it lie, and swung round to the center where their friends were struggling. The right wing also, held by Athenians under Callimachus, won through and came to help. Their leader, who had made such a fateful choice, died fighting bravely, but the rest pressed on. Suddenly, in what had seemed the midst of triumph, the Persians at the center were overwhelmed, and saw the rest of their army already flying. Terror seized them; these warriors seemed more than mortal; they broke and dashed helter-skelter for their ships, while the Greeks streamed after, yelling their war cry, grown so bold now that they grabbed, when they could, the stern posts of the galleys to keep them from launching off.

Afterwards, when tales were told of the battle, men said that as the lines swayed to and fro, and the issue hung upon a hair, in front of the Greek line appeared a mighty warrior, naked as a god, swinging in both hands an axe with a double head. He cheered them on to victory with a voice of bronze, and the Persians fell back in panic; when they had fled, he vanished into air. By his axe they knew that he was Theseus, greatest of the ancient kings, risen from his tomb at his people's need.

There fell, of the invaders, six thousand four hundred men; of the Greeks, one hundred and ninety-two. Every year after, the Athenians held a thanksgiving day for their salvation; and

after the hymns to the gods, a herald stood forth
and prayed for a blessing on the Platæans.

After the battle, when the great disordered
Persian host had scrambled out to sea, and the
fleet lay rocking in the Bay of Marathon, leaving
its dead upon the shore, the Greeks set up a
trophy of the captured arms, rested, and bound
their wounds. But one soldier, who had glanced
by chance to the hilltops of Hymettus, pointed
suddenly and said, "Look! What signal's that?"

It was the flash of a polished shield, winking
into the sun, heliographing a message. Everyone
saw it was speaking not to them, but to the
Persian ships. Somewhere on board was Hippias
the tyrant; he had his spies and his agents still
in Attica. It was all too clear what the signal
meant. "The city is bare of warriors. Sail round.
Now is your chance."

They had fought a hard battle; but there was
only one thing to do: to make the long march
over Hymettus, get back to Athens before the
Persians could reach it, and, at the worst, be
ready to fight again. Few men today, even trained
athletes, would find it possible; the Athenians
only knew they must. Every man who could bear

arms, down to the schoolboys, was here at Marathon; no one was left to defend the walls of Athens but women and children and old men.

So they quick-marched over the hills in their heavy armor, while the Persian ships doubled the long bent coast of Attica with its point at Sunium Head. When the Athenians sighted their city wall, they saw they had won the race. They drew themselves up in line and waited. In time the Persian fleet appeared and stood off shore; they could see the leaders looking out, and thought of the thousands of Medes still left, and how it would go with weary men if the ships came in. Some while the two hosts faced each other, the ships idling on the swell, the Greeks leaning on their spears; then the oars came out, the prows turned southward, the sails were hoisted to the masthead and took the wind. Soon the hulls grew small with distance. The Persians had had enough; they were going home.

The men of Athens went back to their city, and piled their arms about the temples, and praised the gods: Zeus the Rescuer; Athene, Lady of the Citadel; Far-Shooting Apollo; and Ares of the War Cry. The priests stood with garlands on their heads before the ancient shrines, making burnt offerings and pouring out libations from cups of gold; while in the houses the women sang at their work, awaiting their sons and husbands.

When all the deities whom Athens worshiped had had their share of honor, they built on the steep wild slopes of the Acropolis a shrine to Pan. Pheidippides had told them of his vision, and how the friendly god had asked why they forgot him. So they gave him thanks. The Greeks believed in many gods, then and for long after; but the wisest came to think that all the gods were faces of the one God, who comes to men in the form that best meets their need.

IV

THE DRAGON
SPREADS HIS CLAWS

The royal couriers rode to Susa, and Darius heard how his army had been driven back into the sea by a handful of men. His rage was even greater, now, than when the city of Sardis fell. He would leave his vengeance no longer to lesser men. He would go himself.

All over the great empire of the Medes and Persians he sent his messengers to raise fresh troops, and seize in the King's name horses and stores and ships. For three years all Asia was in ferment while the best and bravest of the empire's warriors settled their estates and made ready to march westward.

In the fourth year, the land of Egypt, which
Cambyses had enslaved, rose in rebellion. So
great, by now, was Darius' army, that he declared
he would divide it and fight both wars at once.
But while he was counting on triumph over both
his enemies, a sudden sickness took him; and he
died without having worked his will on either.

Xerxes, his son, succeeded him. He had Darius' pride, without his firmness. Where the father would have known his own mind and let no
one change it, the son was weak and obstinate by
turns, listening now to a good adviser, now a bad.
His uncle, the wise old Artabanes, urged him to
be content with subduing Egypt, and not to try
to push his frontiers into Europe where no past
enterprise had come to good. But Mardonius, his
cousin, ambitious of ruling great lands in
Greece, told him he would be the scorn of the
Ionians if he did not punish the insolent allies
who had helped them to rebel. These Greeks,
Mardonius said, were only a poor scattered
people, often at war with one another, divided
by their mountains; to the Persian might it
would be an easy war, and only cowards would
shrink from it. So Xerxes, having heard what he

wished to hear, turned upon Artabanes. "If you were not my father's brother, you should suffer for your foolish words. Since you are, I will only put one shame on you: When I go to war, you shall stay at home with the women, while I win victory without you. If we do not invade these Greeks, we shall soon have them invading us. Let no man call me Darius' son if I do not give them their deserts!"

So first he dealt with the Egyptians, and bound the land with a heavier chain than Darius had. Then he rode home, and set all his satraps and his generals to get ready for war with Greece.

When he had given his orders, and night had come, he slept and dreamed a dream. He thought he was crowned with a wreath of olive, which sent out branches to cover the whole earth; then suddenly it vanished from his brow. So clear was this vision when he woke, that he called the Magi, his astrologers, to interpret it. They said it meant without doubt that he would rule over all mankind. This pleased him greatly, and he went on preparing for war.

All armies of the past, of the greatest kings, were nothing compared with this that Xerxes gathered. It came from every land of Asia, up to the great barriers of steppe and mountain beyond which all was unknown. One sent him foot soldiers, another horses; a third, provisions and stores; ships came from Tyre and Sidon and Ionia; he also had a store of timber, rafts and pontoons. For Xerxes had formed a great design. Rather than send his main host by sea, where storms might scatter it, he meant to bridge the Hellespont.

This is the strait that runs between two seas and divides Europe from Asia Minor. It is a mile wide; but he swore he would bring his troops across it dry-shod. If he could conquer nature, it would be a little thing to conquer men.

The last thing that happened before he set forth was this. There was among his subjects a rich lord, worth millions in gold and gems, and in lands still more. This man had not only paid his set tribute to the King, but often given him splendid feasts and treasures for his palace—a golden vine with grapes of precious gems, and a golden plane tree, which were the glories of the throne room. Now he offered as a free gift, to show his loyalty, four million gold pieces towards the cost of the war. Xerxes was charmed, and told him he might count himself henceforward among the King's own friends.

When the army was leaving, this man came humbly and begged a favor. Xerxes, who thought he would be asked to accept some other splendid gift, said smiling that he would grant it, whatever it might be. The old lord said, "King of Kings! Your servant has five sons, whom you have called up for the war. Pity, I beg you, my old age, and leave only one, the eldest, to stay and help me. Take with you all the rest; and may you prosper in your enterprise."

But Xerxes answered him in rage, "You wretch! Do you dare to ask your son, when I myself with my own family am going into battle? You are my bondsman; you yourself with your whole household, even your wife if I should choose, are bound to my service. Through the doors of my ears your words have reached my soul, and it is filled with anger. In return for your gifts, I will spare your life and four of your sons; but as for the one you cling to, this shall be your punishment: he shall die, and the two halves of his body shall be nailed to either side

GREECE AND ASIA MINOR
AT THE TIME OF THE PERSIAN WARS

ROUTE OF XERXES' ARMY

MACEDON

Epirus

Thessaly

ÆGE

GREECE

Acarnania

ARTEMISIUM

Ætolia

Locris

Phocis

THERMOPYLÆ

DELPHI

Bœotia

Euboea

PLATÆA

MARATHON

Achaia

Attica

ATHENS
PIRÆUS

Elis

Arcadia

CORINTH

Salamis

OLYMPIA

Argolis

Ægina

PELOPONNESE

TROIZEN

Saronic
Gulf

Messenia

Laconia

SPARTA

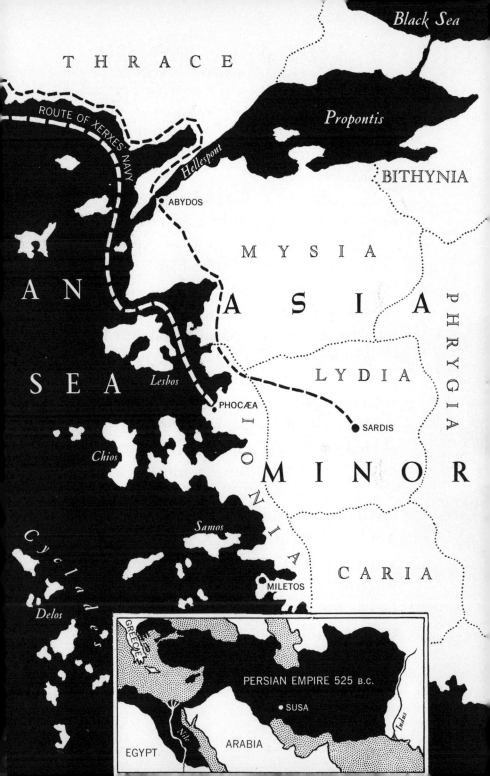

of the city gate when my army marches through it." And this was done. There was no law among the Medes and Persians stronger than the will of the King.

Meantime the builders and the engineers had set about the bridging of the strait. They made a double bridge, held up by two lines of ships. One lane was slung on cables of white flax, Phœnician work, woven to great strength and thickness; the other on huge cables of papyrus, made in Egypt. But when it was just finished, down came a storm (there are many on that stretch of water) and swept both bridges away.

Xerxes was so enraged that even wind and tide should cross his will that he ordered the strait of Hellespont to be scourged with three hundred lashes, and fetters thrown into it, with these words cried aloud: "Wicked water, your lord is thrashing you because you wronged him without just cause. Truly King Xerxes will cross you, whether you will or no. Let no man honor you, you treacherous, evil stream."

The Ionian Greeks, whom Xerxes had forced to follow him, were shocked by this to the very soul. Men believed then that all great waters had guardian spirits, whom one should reverence rather than offend. It seemed to them that by this wild insolence, Xerxes was behaving as if he thought himself a god; "And that," they said, "the gods never forgive."

When the strait had been scourged, Xerxes had all the engineers who had designed the bridge beheaded; then he brought new ones to start again. They had no wish to join the first, and left nothing to chance this time. They used 674 ships to carry the weight of the spans, moored with strong anchors, bow-on to the current of the strait. Each bridge had six cables, two of flax and four of papyrus, joining the ships together. These cables were wound tight around huge capstans, turned by a host of slaves, till they were taut across the water; then thick planks were laid across the cables and lashed together; then a floor of brushwood was strewn over the planks; then earth was shoveled into the brushwood and trampled down. Lastly they raised a parapet along each side, so that the horses should not take fright from looking at the water.

While Xerxes waited, fretful with impatience, he had a tall throne of marble raised upon a nearby hill. Here he would sit and watch his army cross from Asia into Europe, over the humbled strait. At last the bridge was ready; the innumerable army stood beside the shore, in regiments and squadrons and wild un-reckoned hordes. To learn their numbers—for they had been too many to be counted as they marched—he made ten thousand men stand closely in a square and had a line marked round them. When they had gone, the square was filled up again, and so on with all the army. Herodotus says there were 1,700,000 men.

Now they began to cross the bridges, thousand upon thousand: Medes and Persians in sleeved tunics and long trousers, glittering with fish-scale armor; Assyrians with thick black beards, bearing lances and iron-bound clubs; wild Scythians in pointed caps, with leather suits and battle-axes; slender Indians in clothes of brilliant cotton, with bows of cane; Caspians in fur cloaks, with curved scimitars in their sashes; Arabs in white flowing robes; black Ethiopians wearing the skins of leopards and of lions, their faces and their bodies gaudy with war paint, white and red, and on their heads the scalps of

horses with the manes worked into crests; they
were armed with six-foot longbows whose arrows
were tipped with flint. The Chalybians had ox-
hide shields and wolf-spears, and bronze helmets
horned like bulls. From all the lands between
India and the Ægean they had come, even from
the sun-shriveled rocky islands that stand like
dragons' teeth in the Red Sea. As they poured
over the bridges, the under-officers drove them
on with whips, to speed the crossing. There was
not much to choose, in Xerxes' army, between a
common soldier and a slave.

Over the second bridge the cavalry was going;
princes from India, silk clad, on splendid steeds
or in jeweled chariots; wandering desert tribesmen who fought with lassos, and with daggers
to stab the men they threw; sheiks of Arabia
leading their eagle-faced warriors, crossing by
themselves because the smell of their camels
made the horses bolt.

The cream of the whole army were the Persians, marching last to be next to the King.
Their clothes, their weapons and armor flashed
with gold; the rich lords had their favorite slave-
girls carried in litters behind. Last of all came

the royal bodyguard, the famed Immortals, ten
thousand strong, whose spears were balanced at
the butt with golden pomegranates.

After these were led the sacred horses of
Nisæa, beasts towering above the common
height, which no other land could breed, drawing the Chariot of the Sun; for Xerxes had
brought his god along with him, and the floor of
the holy chariot had never been touched by foot
of man. Only the invisible deity might ride
there, and even the charioteer must walk beside
his milk-white team.

Last of all came King Xerxes' chariot, plated
with gold and ivory, and worked with scenes of
victorious war. When all the host had crossed,
then Xerxes would mount it. High plumes shook
over the giant horses' heads, making them look
yet taller; the charioteer was a Persian prince.
In a holster stood the King's gold-bound long-
bow and his quiver netted with precious gems.
He had a curtained litter too, to rest in when he
was tired.

But now he sat upon his hilltop throne, to see
the sight. From this lofty height, it seemed that
a swarm of glittering ants was creeping on

threads across the water, and spreading out upon the plain. Above him was the great arch of the sky; below, the waters of the strait he had bridged so proudly flowed on towards the vast untamed seas; beyond were far mountains, shimmering blue with distance; and beyond again more mountains, unknown and lost in cloud. Suddenly there fell upon him awe of the eternal gods; he felt the measure of man's littleness, who sees himself the center of earth and heaven, yet passes like a flower. He covered his face with his embroidered sleeve, and tears flowed from his eyes.

His old uncle Artabanes who, partly forgiven, had been allowed to come thus far with him, approached and asked him why he wept. Xerxes replied, "A sudden pity came on me, for the shortness of man's life, when I thought that out of all this great multitude not one will be alive in a hundred years." His uncle, who knew him for a man of moods (had he not thrown gold into the Hellespont to make amends for scourging it?), said soothingly, "There are worse things than death, or men in deep sorrow would not wish for it. Better a short and happy life, than one which great troubles make to seem too long." The truth was that he was still full of doubts about the war; but he thought he had said enough.

The moment of truth passed by; the army crossed, and was drawn up on the farther shore; and Xerxes in his chariot drove past the massed battalions till he had reviewed them all. Then he boarded a galley and was rowed past all the ships; for he had assembled a vast fleet as well. Now he had left the mountain he seemed great again, a king of kings, and his pride returned. When he was resting in his tent, he said, "Send me Demaratus."

Demaratus came. He was the last man one might expect to see in Xerxes' tent. He was a Greek, born free; and not only a Greek but a Spartan; and not only a Spartan but a king. And he was here of his own free will.

This was his story. It was the law in Sparta to have two kings at a time, and often they were rivals, or got on badly. So it had been with Demaratus and Cleomenes. Cleomenes was cruel and unjust; they had often quarreled. To make things worse, Demaratus had no son; the heir

in his own line was a cousin, who hated him too, because they had courted the same girl and Demaratus won her. These enemies made a plot to ruin him; they put it about that he was not the true heir, but that his mother had brought up a Helot's child and passed him off as royal. And to this crime Cleomenes added one much greater. He knew the Spartans, being in doubt, would send to Delphi to consult Apollo's oracle. So he went to the Pythia, the prophetess, whose sacred trust was to speak only as the god inspired her, and offered her gold to declare the charge was true. He was not her king; Delphi was in another country; but she was moved by greed and took the gold. The oracle declared against Demaratus; the Spartans deposed him and made his cousin, the plotting heir, king in his place. Not many years later, Cleomenes went mad and killed himself; and some said it was the anger of Apollo, whose shrine he had defiled.

As for Demaratus, shame and his rivals' taunts tortured his pride till he felt his life past bearing. He left the country, swearing that all Sparta should suffer for his wrongs. He went to Darius, who was then still reigning, and offered to fight for him against Greece.

In later times, Darius might have thought, "If this man can betray his own people, why not me?" He did not think so, because revenge and blood feud were acknowledged everywhere as the rights of a wronged man. It was five hundred years and more before Christ taught forgiveness. Demaratus was made welcome at the Persian court and did not feel himself a traitor. He had shaken the dust of Sparta from his feet; having taken Darius as his overlord he served him loyally, and Xerxes after his death. Like Hippias, who was here too in Xerxes' train, he hoped to be given back his throne if the Persians won. Now he stood in the royal tent, at his master's bidding.

"Demaratus," said the King, "you are a Greek, from the strongest land in Greece, or so you tell me. Do you think your people will resist such a host as mine? Surely, even if all these barbarous tribes could be gathered in one army, they could not stand against us; as it is they are divided among themselves, no two lands agreeing. What do you say?"

Demaratus, who, feeling no shame at what he did, had kept his pride, said calmly, "Do you want flattery, my lord, or truth?" All Spartans were plain speakers, and their customs did not change.

"The truth," said Xerxes. "Speak and fear nothing."

"So be it, my lord. You will find I have not lied to you. In our land we have lived with want and hardship; courage has been our only friend. With her help we have driven out want and avoided slavery. The Greeks are all brave in the Dorian lands; but I speak now of the Spartans. First, they will never accept your terms which would bring them into servitude; second, they will fight, though every other people in Greece submits. Do not ask me their numbers, or if there are enough to stand. If they were only a thousand strong, they would meet you in the field."

Xerxes was not angry. These words seemed so wild that he only laughed. "That might be," he said, "if they had, like my men, a single master whom they feared more than the enemy. They might be lashed with whips into such an unequal fight. But tell me no such folly of men who are free to choose. However, don't fear; I know that you meant no harm."

Demaratus answered, "Lord King, your father and you have sheltered me, a homeless exile whom the Spartans robbed of rank and honor. You may judge if I speak from love of them. You asked me for the truth, and it is this. One Spartan alone is brave; but a Spartan army is braver. They are free, yes; but not in everything. Our ancient law is their master; they fear it more than your subjects fear even you. It never changes. It forbids them to run from any odds at all; it commands them to win or die. You asked me; I have spoken. Unless you bid me, I will never speak again, only pray the gods to grant you victory."

Xerxes smiled to himself. He trusted his loyalty, but not his sense; so he sent him away with kindly words.

V

THE LION
IN THE GATEWAY

The army of the Medes streamed through the northern passes. The peoples who, before, had given earth and water to Darius, now had to feed it when it passed their way. It was like the settling of a cloud of locusts, which leaves the land black and bare. It is said that even the very rivers were drunk dry by the passing hordes.

In Macedon, young Alexander was ten years older. He had been king for some time, with the lives of his people in his own charge; and he had seen what his old father had known before, the horrors of sack and slavery. Neither the pride of youth nor its quick thinking would help him now. His father had given earth and water; he was suspect himself already about the vanished embassy. He saw no hope in resistance, and carried out Amyntas' pledge, feeding the army from his lands, and leading his warriors in the train of the King. But he thought in his heart that a man compelled owes no debt of honor; and he cherished his Greek blood still.

Xerxes had wept to think that none of them all would be there in a hundred years. But to the Greeks of the south, destruction seemed much closer. They met in war council, those who had defied Darius' heralds, and talked of the passes through the mountains, debating which could be held and how. When they had agreed upon the best and strongest, they chose the men to hold it; and it seemed there could be no choice but one.

Down in the fertile land of Sparta, where a free man lived harder than a serf elsewhere, the vanguard gathered under a new untried king. For centuries they had lived by the ancestral laws; enduring cold, hunger and weariness, never questioning an order, never changing the custom, silent in pain. All arts and graces they had laid aside, to be in one thing supreme. Now their hour struck. They put on their tunics of scarlet wool which showed no blood in battle, took up their long spears and their heavy shields, and set their faces to immortality.

North and east they marched over the mountains, speaking shortly, covering the miles, and, if they were tired, not telling their nearest friend: a king and a royal guard, the number fixed by custom, three hundred men. The young man at their head talked least of all. He had much to think of: the fate before him, and the fate that had made him king.

Cleomenes was dead, and a shame had passed from Sparta. At the end, when drink and rage had crazed him, they had had to chain him like a rabid dog, till he had got a knife by threatening some poor Helot, who feared him even in his bonds, and slashed himself to ribbons. The kingship had gone back to the house of his half-brothers, who should have had it all along.

His father, King Anaxandridas, had had a wife he dearly loved; but they had no children. After some years, the ephors came to him and said, "Since your wife has given you no heir, you must divorce her, and choose again." The king was angry; even Spartan obedience would not stretch to this. "She has never done me any wrong," he said, "and she is dear to me. I will not do it." But they left him no peace, accusing him of putting his own happiness before his people's good; so at last he said, "Nothing will make me turn my wife away. But to satisfy the people, if you like I will marry a second. She must have a house of her own; I will not have my wife made wretched, who has been nothing but kind to me." So he married this second wife, and she had a child, Cleomenes. From the first he was a cruel, bullying boy, not quite right in the head. Very soon afterwards, the king's real wife had three fine sons, one after the other. But as the customs in Sparta never changed, when the father died Cleomenes was made king. He was the eldest.

The first of the half-brothers, Dorieus, could not bear it. He was the bravest and strongest of all the Spartan youth, admired by everyone; he had been sure in his heart that when the time came, they would never pass him over for Cleomenes. In bitterness he called for volunteers to found a colony, and sailed away with his friends, never to return. Cleomenes died young; but Dorieus was dead already in a foreign land. So the kingship had passed to the second brother of the three. It was he who was leading the vanguard northward. He was called Leonidas, or Lionheart, as we might say.

Now was his chance to bring back their house to honor, and give his mother the pride she had been robbed of for so long. But, as he turned to see the last of Sparta between two peaks, his thoughts were on something even greater.

When the news of the great invasion reached them, the Spartans had sent again to Delphi, asking Apollo how to save their land. The priestess Cleomenes had bribed was gone, found out long since and disgraced; the Pythia in her cave had spoken in the true trance of the god. The priests whose office it was to interpret her wild and wandering speech had put it, as the custom was, into sense and verse.

> *O Spartans, an enemy comes*
> *like the might and terror of Zeus;*
> *No man can withstand him,*
> *though brave as a lion or a bull.*

One of two things must be;
your glorious city must perish,
Or else you must mourn a king,
a son of Herakles' line.

All his life long, before he was old enough to know the meaning of death, Leonidas had been taught he must despise it. Since he had been a warrior, he had trained himself not even to think of fear; it was better, in Sparta, to be a homeless dog than a coward. But he, who had never dreamed that he would one day be king, had dreamed still less that Apollo would choose him, as great kings had been chosen in the ancient days of the heroes, to offer his life as a sacrifice to save the people. He marched alone with his thoughts, belonging already to the god.

They had given him three hundred men. Sparta could have raised as many thousand, and more. The ephors had told him that the rest ought not to follow till the sacred days of the Carnean feast were past; that was the custom. Though he was king, he was master only on the battlefield; it was not his part to ask questions. When they came to the Isthmus' neck, they saw a great wall being built of whatever lay to hand;

stones and timber and sand-packed baskets, and
Spartans overseeing the work. The Greeks from
the other lands were saying to each other that
this was where the main Spartan force would
take its stand; that they were sending this small
troop to make a show, but would not risk their
manpower so far from Sparta, which must be
saved whoever else should be overrun. But
Leonidas and his three hundred marched on to
the north. They had had their orders, and there
was no more to say.

In one thing, for once, when he chose his men,
Leonidas had changed a custom. The king's
guard had always been drawn from young men
eager to prove themselves in battle; it was the
prize of an Olympic victor to fight at his right
hand. But he had taken out all those too young
to have married and had children, and filled
their places with men who had. The Spartans
were few among many Helots, no Spartan ever
forgot it; next to war, it was a man's first duty to
carry on his line. His men had understood; it
was odds against their coming home again. Well,
death would come when it came; what mattered

was how one met it. They had had their orders; to find a pass which was called Thermopylæ, and hold it. That was all. So they marched on, dour and enduring, over the Isthmus into lands they had never seen: the king obeying the ephors, the Spartans obeying the king; and the Helots, who carried the baggage and the heavy arms, obeying each his Spartan master. They had breathed in obedience from the hour of birth.

The army of the Medes poured southward, over Thessaly and into Malis, till the squeeze of the mountains and the shore narrowed it down to one great column, between the crags and the sea. The road got steeper and narrower, till it was no more than a cart track where two carts could not safely pass each other, for fear of the drop below. In this bottleneck, the flow of troops slowed to a trickle. Xerxes, taking his ease in his curtained litter screened from the noonday heat, fretted impatiently. There was now no advance at all. He could hear milling and noise ahead; shouts from the men in front to those behind, which sank to muttering when it neared the royal ear. He parted his curtains, and asked the captain of his guard the cause of the delay.

"Mighty King," came the answer, "the pass ahead is blocked."

"Then send the Nubian slaves to clear it." He was getting angry.

"Sire, it is manned. It must be the Greek advance guard."

At this the King got out, and walked upon the hillside to see for himself. "That handful?" he said scornfully. "Send a spy up the mountain, to see how many more there are of them, and what they are doing. And put my throne up here. I will sit and watch while the pass is forced. Make haste, before it is over. What is this place?"

"It is called the Hot Gates, Sire, from some warm springs nearby. In the Greek tongue, it is Thermopylæ."

Xerxes looked down to the narrow road. A rough stone wall had been piled across it; he could see small figures moving, and a glint of bronze. It was too far to see more.

After a while the spy came back. He did reverence in the dust before the King, and told what he had seen. When the King frowned disbelievingly, he said, "My lord, I swear. With these eyes I saw it. On my life."

"Combing their hair, you say? The guard before the pass? Holding sports, running races, combing their hair?" He laughed loudly; his courtiers hastened to laugh too. "It is the women they have sent us, while the men sit weaving at home."

The courtiers laughed again; but somewhere Xerxes felt a silence. He turned, and saw Demaratus, and beckoned him near. Demaratus saluted with his hand. The Spartan was not born who would kiss the dust before any mortal; and Xerxes, not wishing to kill this useful man, had never asked it. "Well, Demaratus? You, if anyone, can tell us what this means."

"O King, I told you in the beginning about my people. You laughed; but it has happened as I said. I will tell you the truth once more. These men have come to fight us for the pass. For that they are making ready. It is their custom before battle to dress their hair, as if for a festival. The games are to limber them for combat. Those whom you see are the bravest men in Greece. Conquer them, and you will conquer all."

"But," said Xerxes, trusting his ears no more than his eyes, "how *can* so few resist us?"

But Demaratus had already talked overlong

for a Spartan. He said, "Call me a liar, if it does not happen as I said."

By this time, the Persian spies had climbed the heights and seen the whole Greek force, such as it was; three hundred Spartans, and the allies they had called on from lands near by, in all about seven thousand men. It seemed to Xerxes like a child going into battle with a wooden sword. "Let them cool," he said, "from looking at our army. Why lose any men over what we can have for nothing? When they see our numbers they will run away."

He sat there for five days. When on the fifth he found that they had not gone, he began to be angry. "Send out the regiments of the Medes and Cissians," he said. "Take them alive, and bring them here before me. I do not like their impudence."

The Medes and Cissians, in trousers and fish-scale armor, with rich embroidered turbans on their heads and daggers at their thighs, rushed eagerly into battle, impatient after these days of idleness to clear the way. The great bows which were their pride were not much good in the narrow pass; they had to use their spears. But the Greek spears were longer; the Medes, though they were many, had no room to spread and out-flank them; the foremost ranks met hand to hand, and the Medes began to fall. They fell so thickly, as the day wore on, that the rear ranks coming on had to climb over heaps of dead, which served the Greeks for a rampart. Night fell, and the holders of the pass had not given an inch of ground.

Next day King Xerxes said, "It seems I have many soldiers, but few warriors. Let us end this business. Send in the Immortals."

The proud crack troops of the royal household sounded their trumpets and marched towards the pass. They got their name because there were always just ten thousand; when one died or grew old, a picked warrior took his place. To be chosen was the highest honor. Now they were to display their courage under the very eyes of the King. They were famous throughout the Empire; when the Greeks before the pass fled from their onset as if in terror, it was no more than they expected, and they gave chase at the run. But suddenly, in the jaws of the rocky way, the Spartans whipped round like one man, leaping at the unready Persians with their long spears. It was a ruse they used on troops who did not know them. No Greek would have believed in a fleeing Spartan; but the Immortals learned too late. They fell back, leaving their dead behind.

All day the battle raged. The Persians, thinking the Greeks had simply lost their nerve and then recovered it, fell into the trap again and again, thinking each time that they were broken at last. It is said that Xerxes, watching from his throne, thrice leaped to his feet in his anger and dismay.

Night fell. The Persians retired to camp without a foothold won; the weary Greeks rested and dressed their wounds, and saw the innumerable watchfires of the Medes scattered through the darkness, like the stars of a still, clear night, so many that they light the earth.

Next morning Xerxes said, "Today must see a finish. They must be worn out by now. They cannot face fresh troops through another day." But though the new companies were driven with whips into the pass with its teeth of iron, they could not force it, and its throat was choked with the dead.

It was new to Xerxes to be thwarted by men over whom he had no power. His mind was at a stop. He had not ships enough to fetch off this great horde by sea, even if he could have borne the shame of it. He sat in his lamplit tent, with his gold-worked armor glittering on the tent-pole, and the men who served him walking soft-footed, lest his smoldering rage should turn their way. Time was against him; beyond the pass all Hellas would be rallying for war, the feuds he had trusted to flaw their strength set aside in the common danger, and this defiance at Thermopylæ to give them heart. He sat powerless, the greatest king on earth.

It was then that one of his generals asked at the door for leave to enter; he had good news, he said, for the King. When he came in, a man of Greece was with him.

The man bowed down to the ground and kissed it. It was a small thing beside what he had come to do. He said, "I am Ephialtes of Trachis. A poor man, but your well-wisher, mighty King." His eyes stole greedily about the tent, lingering on gold cup or jeweled sword belt.

"Will great Xerxes be my friend if I show him how to take the pass?"

Xerxes signed him to get up. After all, the gods of Persia had not failed. They had sent a traitor.

"Greek," he said, "if you do this, I will weigh you with fine gold, and make you the satrap of your people. Well?"

"There is a path, great King, around the mountain there. It is hard to find, but I know the country. I can guide your soldiers, to take them from behind."

The King said to the guard beside him, "Bring me Hydarnes, Commander of the Immortals." He turned back to the smiling man. "I will trust you, Greek. If you keep faith, you shall eat off gold till the day you die. If you lie, and lead my men into a trap, then you shall drink your gold, poured molten down your throat."

Ephialtes bowed again, and answered, "The King shall see that I am his friend."

In the dark of the night, Hydarnes assembled his Immortals. The word was passed in whispers, lest the Greeks should hear, for the air was windless and still. With muffled weapons, treading softly, they followed Ephialtes up through the oak woods by a track that twisted between the trees.

The night wore on. In the Greek camp, at the first gray of daybreak, an old man, crowned with laurel, stood before an altar of turf and stones. He was the soothsayer-priest Megistias, who had risen early to take the omens for the day. He had made the sacrifice of a kid; now when there was light enough he stooped over the entrails, looking for the signs that he alone could read. "Ruler of gods and men," he prayed, "All-Knowing Zeus, make clear your servant's eyes. Speak to us, Zeus the King."

The light increased. He saw what was to be seen, and covered his face.

"Zeus, I grow old. Keep me from error. Let them not say to me, 'Prophet of evil, it was you who took our hope away.' "

He looked again. The signs were there unchanged. "Even so, All-Knowing and All-Just. It is given only to the gods to live forever. And honor you have not taken from us."

Then he went to tell Leonidas.

The young king heard him calmly. For himself, it was no news. Now that he knew the death omens were for all of them, he felt no pity for his men. To fall bravely in battle was the end that every Spartan prayed for. They would die far from home; but with all Hellas to watch and honor them. Theirs was the greatest fortune of the warrior, an everlasting fame.

Already the news was spreading through the troop. As the tops of the mountains caught the first pink glow, down in the dusk of the pass the Spartans sat upon the rocks above the sea, and combed out their long fair hair. Though some had hoped that they might fight and live, that the army of Sparta might come up in time to save them, none spoke of it to the others. They made the war jokes that they had learned as boys, jokes with few words. One said, "These Persians boast that their arrows fly so thickly they darken the sky. We're in luck; we'll have our fight in the shade." So they talked, warned of their death but not of how it would reach them, while it crept close above them on the mountain track.

Leonidas was a well-trained soldier. He had not taken his position without surveying the ground. He had learned of the path, and put a guard on it, drawn from some allied troops, the Phocians. In the still, calm night there had hardly been a sough of wind in the oak trees. Long before the Persians could come near, the Phocians had heard the rustle of dry leaves underfoot. But they were simple men, all volunteers, small landowners and tradesmen mostly, not reared to war like the Spartans. When the first arrows reached them, they thought some Persians had come up here on purpose to give them battle; so they looked for a place that would give them the advantage of the ground. They backed towards the mountain crest, where they could better defend themselves, and learned their folly too late. The many-footed rustling came no nearer; they heard it pass on round the mountain side. The Immortals would waste no time upon the Phocians, when the path was open to Thermopylæ. By the time of the first sunlight, they were above the pass.

Now the end was plain. Leonidas called the allied commanders, told them that all was lost, and released them from their duty. They thought of their homes down south, left undefended, and took his offer; what else was left to do? When they saw that the Spartans made no move to go, they thanked Leonidas for taking the dangerous rearguard and retreating last.

"Retreat?" he said, as if the very word were strange. "The people of Sparta ordered us to hold the pass."

"But," said the allied captains, "the pass is lost, as you have said. You will disband six thousand men, and stand here with three hundred?"

"We have had our orders," said Leonidas. He said no more; he had been taught that enough words were enough.

The allies marched off; but one contingent stayed behind. The little force of the Thespians, seven hundred, had caught an inward fire from the men of Sparta, and stayed to share their glory and their death. The Helots stayed too, patient in servitude; or remembering at the last perhaps, after all the years of bondage, that they were Hellenes still.

When all this was settled, and the stream of Persians on the mountain side was drawing near, Leonidas turned to the priest Megistias. "You too, good old man. Pack up your sacred vessels: there is no time to lose."

Megistias shook his white head, with the laurel wreath upon it. "A god is in this place, and will not let me go. Father and son, we have been seers since the wars of Troy. My son has the Sight from me; I shall send him home to serve the shrine. This arm of mine has strength still to hold a shield."

"So be it," said the King. They stood and watched the light creep down the mountain, touching the armor of the Immortals and making it flash like gold. On another hill, it caught the columns of a little temple. Megistias said, "That is the shrine of Herakles, son of Zeus, from whom you are descended. Here in this land, when his mighty tasks were done, he lay upon the pyre and was released from toil. Look how it glows like fire."

The sun sailed clear above the islands into a cloudless sky. Leonidas turned his face to it; he would never see it rise again. Evening would come for other men, and the long night; but neither sunset, nor night, nor age, nor time's forgetfulness would fall upon Leonidas and his Three Hundred.

He called his men to battle order, and led

them outside the wall. When the Persians were within hailing distance, Hydarnes halted the Immortals. A warrior of renown himself, he honored courage in other men. "They have done enough," he thought; "perhaps I can persuade Xerxes to mercy." He called out in bad Greek, "Deliver up your arms!"

Leonidas leaped upon a rock and raised his spear. His shout re-echoed from the cliffs, like the roar of the lion, his namesake. "Come and get them!"

Till now the Greeks had been concerned to hold the pass. Now that they went forth resolved to die, they charged forward among the Persians, who fell in heaps. Behind them the captains of the squadrons, armed with whips, thrashed on the hindmost. Many were pushed over the rocks into the sea, and drowned there; many were trampled by the troops coming up behind; no one heeded the dying. The Greeks, when they found themselves hemmed in on every side, drew all together on a hillock, fighting back to back. By now their spears were shattered; but they still hacked down the Persians with their swords.

Here fell Leonidas, fighting till his last breath: they fought the Persians for his body, as the heroes did for their fallen comrades before the walls of Troy. When even their swords were broken in their hands, they fought with their teeth, their fists and nails. At the end, when it was over, Spartans and Thespians lay heaped together, covered with arrows and with javelins, as thick as fallen leaves.

The Helots had different fates. Some were killed, fighting with masters who had won their loyalty; some were taken by the Persians to be their slaves, but later may have got away; others escaped up the steep sides of the pass, to live out their lives in freedom. We know that some were saved; for Herodotus took care, he said, to learn the words and deeds of the Spartans; and no one else was left to tell the tale.

After all was still but the kites and vultures swooping to their meal, came Xerxes to view the battlefield. The Persian warriors looked with respect upon the dead; but he, who had not shared the danger, spitefully had the body of Leonidas beheaded and hung upon a cross. This baseness was remembered against him ever after.

Till now the Greeks had only hated him out of fear; now they despised him. He had been sometimes noble, sometimes merciful; and he had lost two brothers in the battle; he might have lived down the mean revenge, if he had taken it on another man. It was Leonidas' glory that threw so black a shadow. So he avenged the insult, even in death.

Where he had fallen, the Greeks put up afterwards a tall stone lion, which stood for many centuries. That coast has changed over the years; the sea is further out; Thermopylæ is a narrow gate no longer; but people still go as they went in that first year, to see the place. Over the grave-mound of the Three Hundred these words were written:

You who pass, bring word of us to the Spartans.
Here we lie. We obeyed their orders.

VI

THE FLOWER
OF THORNS

For four days, at Thermoplyæ, they held the land road from the north. But there was the sea road also.

Most of the Greek states bordered somewhere on the sea, and many of those who had defied the Persian heralds had now sent ships. But just as the Spartan infantry excelled all others, so did the Athenian fleet. Almost half the total force of three hundred-odd ships belonged to Athens. In command was the man to whom her navy owed its being, Themistocles.

This man had held his own among the tough and tangled politics of Athens, where they were even more of a cutthroat struggle than they are in most places now. Often the shrewd man came off better than the good one: and half a lifetime in this school had made Themistocles hard and slippery. No one knew better how to look after himself. Yet in his own way, he was faithful to Athens too. Some time before, the state silver mines of Attica had done so well that somebody had proposed a bonus payment to every citizen. Most of them could very well have used the money; but Themistocles, partly by trickery and partly with common sense, had got them to vote it for shipbuilding instead. He was dealing, after all, with the most intelligent people in the world; they had not watched the fate of the Ionians for nothing, and would not buy today at the cost of tomorrow.

So here he was, in command of the fleet; and might have fairly expected to command the whole allied force. There were only ten ships from Sparta; but such was the Spartans' prestige on land, the allies demanded that the Spartan general, Eurybiades, should be supreme commander. Themistocles was an ambitious man, and, like all Greeks, in love with being first; but here he showed the greatness which made him more than a politician. Rather than cause a quarrel in the allied force at such a time of danger, he stepped down, leaving the chief command to Eurybiades, while he himself led only the Athenians.

This made his task much harder. The Spartans always hated to send troops far from home. They were still at work upon the wall across the Isthmus; and that relieving force for which the heroes of Thermopylæ had looked in vain had never marched north at all. There were always the Helots, waiting to rise when their hard masters' backs were turned; yet they had feared to send no men at all, lest the other Greeks, despairing, might make their peace with Persia, and leave them to stand alone. Whether the Three Hundred had guessed at this, no one can say. They asked no questions, obeyed, and died. Experienced seamen like the Athenians could see that the wall would count for nothing, if the Persians got mastery of the sea and could land troops along the coastline; but the minds of the Spartans were set like stone, from never changing their customs; it was hard to drive a new thought in.

Themistocles knew this; he knew the huge Persian strength; and before his fleet left home he had given orders for Athens to be emptied, if it could not be held. A copy has been found, inscribed on marble, of all his plans for this evacuation. They were well-organized and thorough; as they had need to be, before the end.

Before the Greek fleet sailed to the coastal waters off Thermopylæ, they had had good news. The Persian ships had been caught in a four-day gale; many had been sunk or driven ashore. The hopes of the Greeks had soared, until they sighted Xerxes' navy. The wrecks were nothing, out of so vast a force; it was still the greatest fleet on earth. The Greeks were appalled; it was beyond their worst imaginings. There began to be talk among the allies of leaving their ships abandoned on the beaches, and marching home by land; and the Spartans seemed ready to agree.

Themistocles was desperate. Once back on shore, the Spartans would be off to crouch behind the Isthmus wall, where they would fight, no doubt, to the death for Sparta, but would leave the rest of Greece to shift for itself. Just as he was at his wits' end, an embassy asked to see him.

These men were Eubœans, from the big island just off shore. If the Greek fleet gave up, their land would be the first to be overrun. Perhaps they had heard rumors about Themistocles and his past; at all events, he was the man to whom they offered a huge bribe in gold if he would keep the ships there long enough to cover the flight of the Eubœans to the mainland, before the Persians came. They had chosen the right man, for Themistocles did not hesitate. He took the money.

Certain things need to be remembered about this. Gift-taking was in Greece a very ancient custom. Friendships and alliances were sealed with it in heroic times. Kings gave and received rich presents from each other and from lesser men, repaying them with favors; it was all done in state, and in the open. It was not such a long step from this, when the kings were gone, to bribing public men. Though this was not considered nearly so reputable, few of them were above it; they were hated only if they were too rapacious, or prepared (like the traitor of Thermopylæ) to do something infamous in return. Those who were known never to touch a bribe were so rare that they became quite celebrated.

One such was Themistocles' old enemy and
rival, Aristides the Just. Themistocles, whose
record in bribes was a good deal over the odds,
had found this probity of Aristides' a great an-
noyance, but had managed at last to get him
exiled from Athens and confined to his country
estate.

Now here was a splendid sum in gold, about
$10,000 by today's reckoning, offered Themis-
tocles for doing just what he wanted, himself,
to do. It could not have come at a better time.
He took a sixth of it, which was still a good
round sum, and sent it quietly to Eurybiades
the Spartan. It was a small private gift, he said,
from himself and the Athenians; would Eurybiades in return help him keep the fleet together?

He had sound guesswork to go upon. In
Sparta, by ancient custom, trading was still done
by barter, or with the cumbrous long bars of
iron which had been legal tender before money
was coined. It took a whole cartload of these to
buy anything much. When Spartans got away
from home, and found out what could be had for
a handful of silver, they would lose their heads

and their greed became a byword. Eurybiades was no exception; the bag of gold quite dazzled him. Faced with the enemy he would have died a hero; but this he could not resist. After he had given the fleet orders to stay off Eubœa, nobody else gave trouble except the leader of the Corinthians. Themistocles saw him in secret, and bought him off rather more cheaply than the Spartan, as his rank was less. All the rest of the money the Athenian kept himself, reckoning, no doubt, that he had earned it. There was at least a chance, now, of saving Athens.

When the Persians saw, off Artemisium, this small fleet waiting, they made merry as if victory were already won. But they did not sail out at once; they wanted first to get the enemy surrounded. While this was going on, with the main force idly standing by, they saw, astounded, the Greeks prepare to attack.

"Have they gone mad?" said the Persian captains; and got their ships under way. But the Greeks, when they saw them coming, rowed their fast war galleys into a tight clump, the bows turned outward, the sterns backed into a ring: a shape like the petals of a sunflower. For-

ward of each ship stood her fighting men, with
bows and javelins; it looked a thorny blossom,
and the Persians paused, in no haste to pluck
it. The Greeks all waited. The Persians were
sailing round them, the better to cut them off.
Before long there were plenty of Persian ships
passing them broadside on. There was a shout
of command, passed on around the flower-head;
out darted its spiky petals, as the rowers bent to
their oars. The Greek ships flew on, each mark-
ing down a Persian one; churning a bow wave
at its prow was its great oak ram, made solid
with the keel and thrusting out before it, carved
with some fierce heraldic face of dragon or ram
or boar. They were practiced at turning in narrow waters; speedy and neat, they shot to their
prey like well-aimed spears. The Persian ships
staggered at the thrusts; the planks started,
water poured in, the warriors had to bail instead of fighting. Shouting in triumph, the
Greeks threw out their grappling hooks and
dragged the wallowing hulks towards them;
they cleared the decks with their hurled javelins,
and leaped aboard.

The fight lasted all day. It was no clear victory, for the mass of the Persian fleet was still behind, though it could not get near, in the strait, to use its strength. But when the dark put an end to fighting, the Greeks had captured thirty ships; the Persians had limped back disordered to their base; and the scout ship, which had stood off to watch the land, brought word that at Thermopylæ they were still holding the pass.

That night a storm got up. The Greek ships were in shelter; but a Persian flotilla had been sent round the long island of Eubœa to trap them in the strait, and was caught in open water. Driven onto a harsh lee shore, every vessel was broken on the rocks. At daybreak the Greeks saw wreckage and dead men floating on the tide, and remembered how an oracle had bidden them pray to Boreas, the god of the northwest wind.

The next day, and the next, the two fleets met again; each time the fight broke off at dusk with the Greeks still undefeated. But on the third day, the scout ship came in to say it was all over at Thermopylæ, and the Persian armies were pouring through.

Themistocles had known his ships could not hold out much longer; more than half were damaged. He warned the Eubœans that he had done all he could; any stock they had still not got away had better be slaughtered to feed the army, rather than let the Persians use it. The fleet could stay no longer; the Greek ships turned their prows to their own narrow seas.

It was midsummer. The Persians stripped the vineyards and the fields of all that ripened. Some poor mountain men, whose families were starving, came into the enemy camp, ready to chop wood and carry water, even there, for a little bread. King Xerxes, when he heard of them, called an interpreter and asked them what they thought the Greeks in the south would be doing now. He did not get the answer he expected. The peasants scratched their heads and said that this was the month of the Olympic Games.

They tried, in their simple way, to explain the Games; how they were held every four years, to honor Zeus the King of Heaven, whose throne was on Mount Olympus; how athletes traveled from all over Greece to the Elian plain, even through states their city might be at war with, protected by a sacred truce. They told of the chariot race, the foot race and the wrestling; the pancration, the boxing and the sprint.

"And what is the prize?" asked Xerxes, supposing that to bring them all so far, it must be gold enough to make one rich for life.

"They get a wreath," said the workmen, "cut from a wild olive tree."

At this one of the attendant princes (he was the son of wise old Artabanes) was heard to say, "What kind of men have we come to fight, who will do so much for honor alone?"

Xerxes made light of it, and spoke to the young man slightingly. But the thought stayed with him. It was too soon to forget Thermopylæ.

VII

THE GOLD
OF APOLLO

The road to the south was open. Less than a hundred miles away was the hated Athens. Xerxes would lead the main force of his army there himself, and the thought was sweet to him. But there was another, almost as pleasant: he had sent a strong force westward, to plunder Delphi.

The fame of Delphi, holiest of all the shrines, had spread beyond Greece deep into Asia. Its history was so old, it went back before the coming of the Greeks themselves, to the ancient legendary Shore Folk who had worshiped there thousands of years before. Then, said the tales, it had been guarded by a huge dragon-serpent, dark and tremendous, whose coils could entwine a mountain. It had held the land in terror, till the young Apollo, shining and wise, had swum to the shores below in the likeness of a dolphin, the wisest beast in the sea and the friend of man. On the beach he took back his godlike form and strode towards the mountains, till the dragon met him breathing fire. There was a battle that shook the hills; but at last the dragon lay dead, shot with the arrows of Apollo's silver bow. Then the young god went up to Delphi, and took for himself its prophetic shrine. Now a splendid temple stood over its ancient cave; but down below the age-old volcanic cleft still leaked its vapor from the underworld, and filled the Pythia with a holy madness whose ravings were shot with truth. Age after age wise men and kings, the heads of cities and armies, or private men with problems they could not solve, had climbed the olive slopes of the Pleistos valley and the stony mountainside above, to the shoulder where the shrine looked outward to the sea, and the Shining Cliffs soared upward, sheer to the eagle-haunted sky.

All those who came brought offerings; for if it was proper to bring presents to a king, how much more, they thought, to a god. A poor man might bring only a kid, or a pair of doves; but the great rulers gave treasures of such magnificence that they became showpieces of the sanctuary, famous from land to land. Crœsus the millionaire had given a lion on a plinth, all in solid gold, and a golden basin weighing a quarter-ton. Some Greek cities had had to build strong rooms near the temple, just to house their own gifts. It was said that Xerxes had got the list of all these riches off by heart, and could run them off quicker than he could his own. They were, he thought, as good as his already.

The Persian force marched windingly along the stony track that skirted Mount Parnassus. Its guides were Thessalian traitors; they had done it to be revenged upon their neighbors the Phocians, whom they were at feud with, and through whose land the Persians would have to pass; once more revenge was the curse of Greece. Under the bright midsummer sun, on the pale zigzag road, the long dark train coiled round the mountain spurs, with a glitter of shields and helmets, like a huge serpent shifting its shining scales; like the old dragon bright-haired Apollo had freed the land from, in the half-lit dawn of the world.

Just as the sacred isle of Delos had been un-fortified, so was Delphi; its holiness had been its unseen wall. The priests and the headmen of the town knew well that it was nothing to the men who were coming now but a heap of gold for the looting. They did what was second na-ture to them in any time of trouble; they went to the holy cave, to consult Apollo.

A flickering lamplight scarcely broke the darkness. The Pythia sat on her tripod of an-cient bronze; before her the cleft smoked faintly, and smelled of sulphur. The Navel Stone, a meteor flung from some comet's tail in the distant age of the dragon, stood by her swathed in its magic nets; the air was heavy with scents of earthy stone and soot, of burning wood and bay leaves. The Pythia with a leaf of laurel crushed between her teeth, its cyanide juices swimming in her brain, rolled her wild eyes till the whites were showing, and moaned softly to herself, wrestling in her soul with the rising frenzy of the god. But the golden image of Apollo stood straight and still in the shadowy depths of the cave; his wide-open eyes of polished agate looked through them all and beyond.

The Priest of the Oracle lifted his hands in prayer and put the Delphians' question. "Pythian Apollo, far-seer, Lord of the Silver Bow, mighty musician; we are the guardians of your treasure. What shall we do? Bury it in the earth, before the barbarians come here; or carry it off to some other shrine?"

The Pythia's eyes grew fixed. Fierce tremblings shook her from head to foot; she seemed to grow taller; her hair stood upright at its roots, and she cried with a strong changed voice that filled the cave, "Go, man, and leave my goods with me! Without help from you I can protect my own."

The Delphians obeyed. They sent their women and children and old men, with the holy Pythia, down the valley to the port, to take shelter across the water; for the Gulf of Corinth is a narrow sea. But the active men climbed the steep paths above Delphi beside the Shining

Cliffs, hid their belongings in a cave they knew of, and watched among the rocks. No one remained in Delphi but sixty daring men and the Priest of the Oracle.

What happened then, I tell as the Delphians told the story to Herodotus, the historian, a generation later. We can think what we choose; but this is what they said.

As the Persians drew near Delphi, the priest looked out from the holy shrine, where he had stayed alone. On the path before the precinct, a glint of metal caught his eye, which had not been there before. He went to see. There lying in the way before the temple were the sacred weapons of Apollo; the golden sword, the silver bow and quiver, which no mortal hand, even his own, was allowed to touch.

The priest ran to the town nearby, to tell the waiting men of this strange omen. Then they waited together, while the long Persian column drew near along the road. As its head reached sacred ground, there was a deafening crash of thunder, a mighty splitting overhead, a gathering, rumbling roar. Two huge rock pinnacles came bounding from the heights above, and fell

like thunderbolts among the Persians, while
from the inner sanctuary a great war cry was
heard, and a shout of victory.

The Persians fled in headlong terror. After
them came the sixty Delphians, leaping from
their ambush, while the rest came scrambling
from above. They chased the enemy towards the
steep slope by the road, and cut them down or
pushed them over. And it seemed that in the
vanguard, running ahead, were two tall warriors, towering above the height of common
men. After the fight they disappeared. Two
heroes of ancient fame were buried near; and
the Delphians said it was these who had come
to fight, like Theseus at Marathon.

Delphi is an awesome place. The Persians
while still upon the road may not have liked
their mission; and Pan of the mountains worked
his panic easily. The greater the herd, the
mightier his magic grows; it takes a brave man
alone, like Pheidippides the runner, to win his
friendship. All the vast Persian horde fled like
stampeded cattle, down from the brooding
heights with their keen blue air, stumbling and
straggling mile after mile. They did not rally

till they reached the lowlands of Bœotia. The crags from the Shining Cliffs still lie where they fell upon the Persians, half-buried by their own weight in the sacred soil. For a long time afterwards, travelers came there to look and wonder. To all of these the Delphians told the story, as I have told it here.

VIII

THE UNDYING TREE

During all this while, not knowing yet that he would never bring home Apollo's treasure, King Xerxes was marching his army south to Athens.

The Athenians kept up their hopes. They had risked their men and ships at sea; they thought the Spartans would do as much for them. In Bœotia to the north there was good fighting country, in which the strong main force of Sparta could have held the invaders back. But no force had come. The Spartans were at the Isthmus, building their wall, a wall they would hold to the death; it was getting as strong and as high as the wall that shut in their minds.

When the Athenian leaders saw that the Spartans were concerned only for themselves, and would leave the rest of Greece to take its chance, they asked that the allied fleet should be based at Salamis. The straits are called after the big island off the coast of Attica, which is its other shore. Themistocles chose it, so that they could cover Athens while it was being evacuated. There was nothing else for it now.

The Athenians heard the news with grief and horror; but they were not unprepared. They had had two warnings.

At the start of the war, they had sent to Delphi, asking the god what their fate would be. The gray-bearded envoys had gone down into the holy cave, gazing with awe at the Pythia on her tripod throne. Then they had made for the stone benches by the walls; there might be a good while to wait, while the seer muttered and the priest interpreted. But hardly had they sat down, when the Pythia gave a cry and burst into intelligible speech. Though it was wild and broken, they could follow every dreadful word.

"Lost . . . you are lost . . . why do you sit here? No, no, fly—fly to the ends of the earth! Lost . . . lost . . . lost! The head, the body, the feet, all broken, falling. . . . *Fire! Fire!* Fire in a chariot, fire from Syria, fire from the sands. The sacred marble is sweating, dark sweat of blood, on the brow of the god, on the walls . . . dripping, dripping, black on the stones. Away! Run! Away!"

Crushed with despair, they groped their way up to the daylight. There on the steps of the temple they bowed their heads in their hands and wept for their city, Athens of the violet crown. Time passed; but they sat like stones, unmoving. The men of Delphi, moved by their grief, stood round them offering useless sympathy; till an old lord said, "Do not despair, Athenians, till you have prayed to the god for help. Go back to the shrine; take olive branches with you, the sign of supplication; stretch out your hands to him and beg him to relent."

So they wiped their faces—for tears were thought unfitting before Apollo, like rain in sunlight—and plucked the branches and went again. "Apollo, lord," they said, "have pity on our city. We have honored you there with music, and glorified you with the works of our hands. Look kindly on these olive boughs, and give us a better oracle. Or, here we swear it, we will not leave your holy place but stay here till we die. Turn to us, Apollo."

At first there was silence from the tripod. Then the Pythia gave a deep sigh, and spoke.

"Leave hold . . . let go . . . when all is gone, the wooden wall shall stand, safe for your children. Fall back from the horsemen, fall back. Battle will come when the corn is gathered. Salamis . . . holy Salamis. Death at the harvest, death for the sons of women, battle and death."

The Priest of the Oracle turned both these sayings into verse, to be carried back to Athens. Herodotus, in his history, calls the Athenians the true saviors of all Greece, because in spite of this fearful warning they did not surrender or despair.

So the plans of Themistocles, drawn up before he sailed north with the fleet, were put into effect. There was one last omen, which told them to delay no longer. From an age so long

that no one knew its beginnings, there had been
a sacred House Snake under the Acropolis. No
one saw him but the priestess of Athene, who
took him every month a honey cake as an offering. This time she had gone down, she said, as
usual; but last month's cake lay there uneaten.
The ancient guardian had gone away.

So the people filed down to the shore where
the ships were moored, and went aboard by
families and tribes. All the places round had
promised shelter; Troizen across the Saronic
Gulf, the isle of Salamis; even Ægina, a powerful island with whom Athens had been at war
not long before the invasion. But there was no
room in the ships for anything but bare ne-
cessities. The dogs ran howling with grief
through the empty streets; and one, more strong
and faithful than all the rest, swam after his
owners' ship as far as Salamis. His master found
him on the shore, worn out and dying, and
honored him with a tomb which became famous
and gave its name to the place.

If revenge was the curse of Greece, one of its
greatest virtues has always been hospitality. The
refugees were met with warm hearts and open

hands; in Troizen the children were given free places in the schools, and leave to help themselves from the growing fruit and greenstuff. In Ægina, many of the Athenians climbed the hill of Artemis, the wild beasts' goddess, to her temple at the top. From there, one can see Athens across the water.

The great flat rock of the Acropolis, with its shrines and temples, stood out clearly. They could not see the gay-colored friezes of the temples, it was too far for that; but they saw the columns and temple roofs, and, when the sun was right, the flash from their gilded ornaments.

A natural stronghold, almost impregnable, the Acropolis had been a magnet to men in danger, age after age. From here, with their people around them, King Theseus and King Codrus in their day had held off great invasions, saving the Athenians from the Helots' fate. Perhaps even Themistocles could not have got them to forsake it now, but for the last omen of the House Snake; some say, indeed, that it was another of his tricks.

Even now that all Athens stood deserted, the Acropolis was not empty. The priests and priestesses, loyal to the gods whose shrines they guarded, stayed on as the High Priest had at Delphi; and there were others, poor men mostly, for whom their ancient faith in the High City had been too strong. As their forebears had done in Theseus' or Codrus' time, they climbed the ramps with their wives and children, their cooking pots and bedding, and their little stores of food, and built shacks and lean-tos against the temple walls. They had seen already the wooden barricades which the temple servants were building across the gateway. There, they said, was the wooden wall which the oracle had foretold would save them. Themistocles had said that it meant the wooden ships of Athens; but they knew a wall when they saw it; and how could they hope for luck if they left to the barbarians the temples of the gods? So they stayed on, and watched the long lines of refugees trooping down towards Phaleron Bay and Piræus Harbor. When they looked to the north, there was smoke already on the hills as the Persians came nearer, burning and plundering on their way.

Here came the army that had fled from Delphi; their hearts were bitter, and perhaps still not at ease. But now they could join with the huge main force of Xerxes. Down they came from the hills, with the burning farms behind them, and camped before the citadel, upon the Hill of Ares which faces the great gate. Soon the rock stood like an island in the great sea of men; but even so they could not take it. To destroy the barricade, they shot up arrows tipped with burning pitch; the wooden wall blazed up and crumbled to ash; and still the Athenians, unyielding, rolled down column drums and boulders to sweep the Persians from the ramp. But they were only a few; poor ignorant men and unwarlike priests, not like the great royal garrisons of the ancient kings. While they were busy with the gateway, some Persian mountain troops found a way up the cliffs, which had looked too steep to need defending; and then it was all over. Many leaped down the sheer face to death, sooner than fall alive into Xerxes' hands; others, thinking he would respect the temples' holiness (for they had not had the news from Delphi) fled there for sanctuary. The Persians broke in the doors and butchered everyone; then, when they had carried off the sacred treasures, they burned all that was left.

And so, at last, after thirty years of exile, Hippias son of Pisistratus came back to his kingdom.

Next day, when the fires had burned down to reeking charcoal, he went with his exiled lords to the Acropolis. King Xerxes had sent him there, to sacrifice at the altars. Perhaps it was in thanks for victory, perhaps in atonement, like the gold thrown into the Hellespont.

The old man walked up the bloodstained pathway, where once he had ridden crowned with olive, leading the knights on the day of Athene's feast. Here, blackened with fire, were the columns that had been wreathed with flowers; that woman lying in her blood had been a little girl then, singing in the choir. On he went along the Panathenaic Way, where at the festival the most beautiful youths in Athens had ridden shining horses, or led the great white oxen with gilded horns. At last he came to the oldest shrine of all, shared by Athene and Poseidon, the guardian gods of the land. Here was Poseidon's spring; but it was filled with rubble and ashes; here Athene had planted the first of all the olive trees, as her gift to Athens; the leaves were shriveled, the trunk was barkless and charred. He stood and gazed at what he had won back; and what his thoughts were, who can say?

But presently one of his followers exclaimed, and pointed. They looked again at the burned-out tree. There shooting from its roots was a long sprout of green. Overnight it had grown, they say, a foot and a half.

This omen of hope was never forgotten in Athens. If you go today to the Acropolis, you will find, where the sea-salt spring of Poseidon used to flow, only an empty hollow in the rock. But if ever the olive of Athene dies, on the same spot they plant another, in memory of the victory that came after despair.

Another strange tale is told of those days, when the Persians were in Attica.

Demaratus, the exiled Spartan king, was riding along the plain with a friend of his, Dicæus, one of old Hippias' men. Coming towards them along the coastal road they saw a great cloud of dust, such as might have been raised by an army of thirty thousand.

"What troops can they be?" he asked his

friend. "There is not an Athenian left in Attica. Where does this road lead?"

Dicæus said, "This is the Sacred Way. It goes to Eleusis, to the temple of Demeter the Great Mother, and the Hall of Mysteries."

He stared at the oncoming cloud; Demaratus saw that he was pale, and asked, "What is it?"

"Listen!" Dicæus said. "Can you hear music?" He looked at the Spartan, as if he hoped he might say "No." But Demaratus had heard already, from the heart of the moving cloud, a many-voiced solemn chanting; so he nodded his head.

Suddenly the man of Athens wheeled his horse off the road, and made for the slope beside it. Demaratus, following, found him white and shaken, staring at the highway, where still the cloud of dust rose whirling in the air. "This is the month," he said, "for the Procession of the Mysteries. It goes from Athens to Eleusis; and that is the hymn they sing."

They waited. The cloud drew nearer; but no troop appeared within it, the dust was raised by no human feet. In fear they watched, reining in their frightened horses, while the empty dust cloud passed them, filled with unearthly singing. They saw it float high in the air, and change its course, and go blowing across the strait towards Salamis.

At length Dicæus said, "The Great Mother is leaving us, and going to the Athenians. This is a dreadful omen. Shall we tell the King?"

"Are you mad?" said Demaratus. "You would lose your head and no one on earth could save you. Say nothing, and so will I. As for King Xerxes, he is in the hands of the gods."

IX

SALAMIS

But the face of fate had never looked so dark as it did at Salamis, when the Athenians saw the smoke of their burning homes. Now, indeed, the wooden sides of their ships were all the walls they had.

Their last hope hung on a thread, which was almost breaking. For once again the Spartans were thinking of their Isthmus wall. Eurybiades was still supreme commander, and he carried most of the allies with him. Some, like the Corinthians, had their cities beyond the Isthmus: these were the loudest for going home.

Themistocles almost despaired. He alone saw the great strategic chance these straits afforded;

the rest could only see he was an Athenian, who
wanted Athens retaken at whatever cost to themselves. Again and again, in their council of war
in the harbor town, he argued, exhorted and
implored.

"I beg you to change your minds," he said.
"If you leave these straits, you will strike a
deathblow to all Hellas."

Adiemantus, the Corinthian leader, said,
"You are too fond of your own voice, Athenian.
Don't interrupt so often. Remember, the runner who jumps the start gets thrashed by the
umpire."

"Yes, Adiemantus. And if he gets off too late,
he loses. As you will, if you disperse the fleet
today. Have I no right to speak here? We have
made good all our lost ships, and more; out of
these three hundred, two hundred are from
Athens. And do you think ours is the only fate
at stake? Your ships can never beat the Persians
in open water. What of your homes, when they
command the sea? Here in the narrows, where
their numbers cannot be brought to bear, where
we Athenians know every shoal and current;
here is the hope."

Adiemantus said, "It is your own people you

are thinking of, nobody else. And what are they now? What land, what city do you represent? You cannot call a single foot of earth your own. Let him show, Eurybiades, what state he is the envoy of, before he raises his voice in council here."

This was too much. Themistocles started up in rage, and chose his words no longer. "Base-hearted dog! For this we have borne the shock of battle, and kept the barbarians from your city; for this we have thrown into the war every man and boy who can hold a spear; for this we have melted down our treasures to keep the fleet! Yes, we are landless—because we put freedom and honor before stocks and stones. And you, you slimy squid-fish, a sword without a heart—you ask me what country we are masters of! Shall I tell you? Yours, if we choose! With two hundred ships of war and our men aboard them, we have city and country as good as any man's, wherever we like to take them with sword and spear. Eurybiades, I appeal to you. Take station here and fight, or bring all Greece to ruin. And if you will not be persuaded, I tell you this: In the hour you sail for the Isthmus, we take our families aboard and embark for Italy, to found a new Athens there. When the Medes are on you, and you stand alone, then you will call this day to mind."

Eurybiades had a dull and plodding brain; but this speech got home to him. He said, "Our Corinthian friend spoke rashly. No one is making light of the Athenians. There is reason, I don't deny it, in what you say. Gentlemen, I have changed my mind. I propose we engage the Persians here."

At this there was more wrangling; but the Spartan prestige was great, and no one sailed. So they stayed at Salamis, the allies unwilling and uneasy, and before long they saw the ships of the Persian fleet approaching, squadron after squadron: ships of Egypt, of Cyprus, of Cilicia; of Lycia, Caria and Pamphilia; ships of Tyre and Sidon; ships of Ionia, pressed into Persian service. All the shores of Attica seemed lined with them, as thick as driftwood after a storm. And on the land behind was the Persian army, the footmen, the horses, the chariots, darkening the ground. Soon, upon a height beside the place where the strait was narrowest, they saw a tall platform raised, with something at the top that shone. It was the gilded throne of Xerxes, set for him to view the battle.

It was too much for the allies. They came together in an uproar, abusing Eurybiades, who had let the Athenian talk him into waiting here, and giving them like sheep to butchery. It shook him to the soul. He was no Leonidas; no oracle had called him to the sacrifice; was he not betraying Sparta, he asked himself, for the sake of these Athenians: restless and changeful men, too fond of liberty, too full of questions, men who might be a danger some day to the ancient laws? As the noisy debate went on, Themistocles gave up hope of him. The Spartan would give way. Themistocles left them at it, and slipped out on to the waterfront, the voices fading behind him.

He was thinking furiously, as he had had to do often before in the stormy politics of Athens. He thought like a fox who plots his way out of a thicket while the hounds are baying round. Suddenly he knew what he would do. He sent a messenger to his family's lodging not far off, to fetch him his sons' pedagogue.

There is no job today quite like the pedagogue's in ancient Greece. He was not a tutor,
for he did not teach. He was more like a boys'
male nursemaid; he would take them to school
and call for them, look after their wax tablets
and writing sticks and the lyres they used in
music class, and see that they came straight
home, without getting into bad company or
running wild. For this, Greek fathers would buy
a good steady slave.

Athens was a democracy—for its own citizens.
They expected, when laws were passed or de-
cisions taken, to be there and vote, not leave
their thinking to someone they had elected. It
might take half the day; but they had time because all their routine work, at home or business or workshop, was done by slaves. Slavery
was world-wide; it had occurred to no one yet
that it was evil; it was what one did with beaten
enemies if one spared their lives. One can say
for the Athenians that they made better use of
their leisure than other people, and gave their
slaves a better life. Strangers from other cities
used to say, with disapproval, that you could not
tell a slave in the streets of Athens; they were as

well fed and dressed as anyone else. They could complain against cruel masters, and demand to be resold; if they could earn a little in spare time, and save whatever they had cost, they could buy their freedom. Often after good service, the master would make a present of it. Or a slave might be freed as a gift to honor a god.

The slave Themistocles had sent for was called Sicinnus; and he was a Persian. We do not know his real name, for Sicinnus is a slave-name; nor how he lost his freedom: whether he was captured in the war or, perhaps, by pirates as he made a journey. He may well have been better-born than his own master, who was an unpolished, self-made man. But whoever he was, he had been treated kindly, and repaid it with devoted love. Themistocles needed now, as never in his life, someone he could trust in; and he chose Sicinnus. For the next few hours, the future, which is today for us, lay in the hands of a slave.

Themistocles talked quietly to him, telling him what to do and say till he knew the whole plan by heart. When Sicinnus was ready, he slipped off to some secluded beach and took a boat.

Meantime, in his camp on the coast of Attica, King Xerxes too had called a council of war. Over at Salamis, there had been only tired, harassed men in war-soiled armor shouting and banging the table in a wharfside room. Here the great silken tent of the King was pitched by Phaleron Bay with its swarming warships; before the painted central tent pole stood his golden throne. On lower thrones around, in strict order of precedence, sat the tributary kings. Each kept his state, and each was free to offer his voice in council. But there would be no voting; here, only one man's word was law.

With ceremonious form, the matter was put before them. Here were the Greeks, or what was left of them, boxed up in these Straits of Salamis. True, they were in home waters that they knew; but so outnumbered, it could not count for much. If they were let go now, the war might drag on all winter. Should the Persian fleet attack?

To each king in turn, Xerxes sent round his general Mardonius; by this form of courtesy they could speak to a lesser man and remain seated. To each in turn he bowed, and put the question; first to the King of Sidon, then to the

King of Tyre, and so on to the end. Each said "Attack" except Queen Artemisia, the only woman there. She had come with her ships to war, as ruler of Halicarnassus. She was a Greek, yet not a traitor, for her land had been subject to Persia since before her day. These were her words: "Say to the King, Mardonius, from me who have served him well in battle, 'Master, do not fight the Greeks at sea. As man excels woman with the shield and spear, so does a Greek on shipboard excel a Persian. Have you not done your will on Athens? Is not all Greece within your power? Leave them be. They left home without much food, so they cannot hold out long. Make a move as if you meant to attack the Isthmus. That will make them scatter to their homes; then at your leisure you can deal with them one by one.' "

She was a Greek, and knew her own people. She knew, too, the wisdom of Apollo: "Know yourself. A man is only a man. Nothing too much."

King Xerxes liked her; she was one to herself, and he admired the way she spoke her mind. But he did not take her advice; she was the only one who had not agreed with him.

He gave orders to his squadrons, to get ready their ships for war. They were to attack next day.

It was soon after this that his generals brought him news.

"Sire," they said, "a man of our own people has come here in a boat, seeking speech with the King. He says he comes from the Athenian admiral, Themistocles."

"What?" said King Xerxes. He was pleased and interested, rather than surprised. "So! It well may be. A man who made himself from nothing. He likes money, they say. There was a man who liked it at Thermopylæ, or we might still be sitting before the pass. Bring in this messenger."

Sicinnus entered. He did not need telling how to do reverence to a Persian king. He lay flat upon his face, kissing the dust, and crawling forward on hands and knees. It was a thing he had not had to do in Athens, even though he was a slave.

The King said, "You may speak."

"May All-Glorious Xerxes live forever. The

Athenian commander, Themistocles, has sent me to you, King of Kings, unknown to the other Greeks. He is a friend to your cause and risks his life to help you. He sends you this news: The Greek fleet at Salamis is seized with panic. They will not stay to meet your victorious arms; they plan to fly. If you wish for a quick decision, my master says, do not wait till morning, but cut off their retreat this very night. Trapped in the straits, they will fall into confusion; none will resist you; you are likely to see them fighting each other, for many are half-hearted, and will desert to you. That is my master's message."

Xerxes was overjoyed. This was what he had been saying all along. "What does your master ask of me, in return for this?"

"Nothing, Sire," said Sicinnus humbly, "except that after the battle you will remember him."

King Xerxes nodded, smiling. There was no time to lose, and he gave his orders. The captains were to draw up their ships three deep, and close the Straits of Salamis at both ends. They were to take their stations as soon as darkness hid them. A captain who let a Greek ship pass would pay for it with his head.

When his messengers had gone, he looked round again for the Persian in Greek clothes. But the man had gone, without even waiting for a tip.

Night passed. At Salamis, when the stars began to pale before the dawn, the ships from beyond the Isthmus were launched and manned, waiting the word to sail. Once again, in the busy night, the generals had met; once more Themistocles had pleaded. Weary, unwashed, heavy-eyed, they were still debating, held by his dogged insistence, but longing to get away.

Eurybiades said, "This has all been settled, Themistocles. If we wait much longer, we shall lose the tide."

This was just what Themistocles had hoped for, while he played for time. Time had run out, and all was over . . . unless . . . A seaman beckoned him from the door. "Here's a gentleman, sir, just landed from Ægina, says he must speak to you alone."

From Ægina? His heart sank; he had hoped it was Sicinnus. The thought of other business wearied him; but he went to the door. The face that he saw amazed him. It was Aristides the Just, his old enemy and rival, in politics and out, for half their lives. They stared at each other in the faint cold gray of dawn, and neither spoke.

"Well?" said Themistocles at last. "Have you come to thank me for repealing your vote of exile—to each man his due, even to me? You can spare your thanks; I recalled all exiles, when the people left."

"Thank *you?*" said Aristides. His lean stern face, with the well-bred calm Themistocles knew and hated, had aged in the ten lost years. "You knew I was unjustly banished; you did not want me crossing to the Medes with my supporters, like Demaratus the Spartan. How well you know your own nature; how little you know mine."

"Oh, yes!" Themistocles felt the old resentment rising. "We all look shop-soiled beside Aristides the Just."

"So you told the city mobs, till they hated me for giving them honest service. You have grown rich in office. What made you envious of my poverty, unless it was the smell of honor?"

"Did you come all the way from Ægina, just

to say this?" Themistocles looked over his shoulder at the council room; he had troubles enough without this ghost from the past.

"No!" said Aristides. "We are Athenians both. I came to warn you: get ready your ships to fight."

Themistocles smiled bitterly, and pointed at the allied ships. They were quenching the torches and cressets they had worked all night by; the rowers were already at the oars.

"Yes," said Aristides. "I heard that they meant to sail. But they cannot do it. The Persians have both ends of the strait blockaded. With a skillful pilot, I just got through in the dark. Now day is breaking, no living thing can pass."

Themistocles gave a cry of joy, all else forgotten. "Merciful Zeus be praised! If I live he shall have my offering, the freedom of a slave."

Aristides, staring, said, "Was this *your* work?"

"Yes," said Themistocles. "What else was left?"

"I should have known." The stiff old aristocrat almost laughed; it was so like the man. "I forgive you much for this. Well, since our stars

have marked us out for rivals, let us be rivals
still; not against one another, but in battle
against the Medes."

"If we live, we shall be at odds again; but
not today. Give me your hand."

"So long ago this strife of ours began. And
the lovely face we fought for, gone the way of
last year's roses. And neither of us won the
prize."

"No matter now . . . I have it! *You* go to
the captains, Aristides, and tell the news. From
me they'd take it for another ruse to keep them
here; but who will doubt it from Aristides the
Just?"

He went; and at first they doubted even him.
He too was an Athenian, and his famous hon-
esty not known to all of them. But they listened;
and while they listened his news was proved.
The crew of an Ionian ship of Xerxes' navy,
seeing the death-stroke of the Greeks being
prepared, felt the old tie and rowed across to
warn them, facing what must have looked like
certain death whether they were caught or not.
These brave men's action tipped the scales; but
for them, the Greeks might still have been too

late. Now all doubt was over. The commanders
ran back to their ships, and gave orders to strip
for action.

When all was ready, Themistocles addressed
the fleet. "In every man," he said, "there are two
men, one base, one noble; and we shape our
lives as we choose between them. The easy choice
looks cheap; but the man defeated pays as long
as he lives; while he who chooses to be brave
and risk the price of it, will die with glory or
live with honor, seeing his sons inherit freedom
and bow to no master but the gods. "And this,"
he said, "is our choice today."

The Persian ships were at their stations.
Their orders had been to move up in perfect
silence, unnoticed by the Greeks. This was a
long maneuver and had taken them all night.
The men of Athens were well rested; even the
allied crews who had meant to sail had had a
watch off duty. The Persians were weary and
dim-eyed. Knowing they stood to lose their
heads if a Greek ship slipped through, they
were relieved, when the morning lightened, to
see that none had gone. They waited, to watch
the Greeks' terror when they knew their plight.

But instead of panic shouts, they heard a trumpet. The Greeks were putting out of harbor. The oar-banks beat, winglike, gathering speed; the warriors packed the forepeaks. They were coming in to fight.

We have the whole story of this battle, from a man who fought in it. He was Æschylus, first of the great Athenian playwrights, who put it all into his tragedy, *The Persians*, only eight years after. He found it in his heart to pity them.

It showed the Queen Mother of Persia, at home in Susa, awaiting news of Xerxes her son, and praying for his victory. At last the watched-for herald comes; but his news is only of disaster. He tells how the tough, bronze beaks of the Greek ships rammed into the Persian galleys; how at first they held their line, but soon in the narrow straits their numbers jammed and crippled them; they could not turn, while the light, neat ships of the Greeks swooped round and harried them where they chose, till the face of the water was covered everywhere with a flotsam of wreckage and of dead.

No sails were used in that close fight; the ships were driven with oars; yet the winds fought

for the Athenians. They knew the morning breeze blew in from the open sea; they knew it would catch the high Persian ships, and turn them broadside on, while their own, lower and smaller, could hold their course and come straight in to ram.

Aristides the Just did distinguished service. He captured a little island, which the Persians had filled with troops to kill any shipwrecked Greeks who swam ashore. Thanks to him, they were pulled out safe and sound. All Greeks could swim; they were a seaboard people; but the Persians came mostly from places so far inland that they had never seen the sea, before this campaign. This was one reason why they lost so many men, and the Greeks so few.

When the first news came to him that battle had begun, King Xerxes went up the hill to his gilded throne, to watch his squadrons win.

Around him sat his chroniclers, tablets in hand; they were to record the deeds of valiant Persians, to be rewarded after victory. Proudly he watched the great war game open and move before him, not doubting what the end would be. Only little by little, in the milling chaos, the shape of defeat began to form and harden. At first he did not trust his own eyes, but soon he could doubt no longer. He tore his gold-embroidered robes in sign of mourning, and climbed down from the platform. It was as if he left the throne of the known world. He had barely mounted to its footstool; but he had tasted the power and glory during these days in Attica, and now he felt the bitterness. The throne stood empty. So it would stand for a century and a half, till a young King of Macedon, golden Alexander, took it for all Greece.

Two thousand five hundred years have passed since the Greeks threw back the Persians. But a tide in man's life was turned by it, and we feel its motion even today. It was not just a victory against great odds, by men we like for their courage. It was a victory for reason over blind obedience; for free choice over despotic power; for a man's right to be a living soul, not just the tool of a ruler to be used or scrapped at his whim. Not all these things were clear, at first, to the Greeks themselves. Most of them only thought that now they could go home again and live in their own way, that they would not be slaves.

They behaved like themselves, with their own faults and virtues. This was certainly true about Themistocles.

After the Persians had fled from Attica, the Greeks decided it would not be worth while to pursue them north by land; winter would chase them harder; and they guessed that Xerxes would not delay, lest, now he had lost his ships, someone should cut his bridge across the Hellespont. So it was decided. But Themistocles thought it over afterwards, and decided he might make something out of it for himself.

It was now that he and faithful Sicinnus pulled off their most audacious trick. Themistocles counted on the deluded King believing he had meant his disastrous message all for the best. So, as the Persians were packing up their camp to leave, he actually sent Sicinnus back again; and Xerxes gave him audience.

"My master," Sicinnus said, "sends word to the Great King that out of his friendship to Your Majesty, he has stopped the other Greeks from harassing your armies, or destroying the Hellespont bridge to cut you off. He asks you to remember his kind services if ever he is in need."

Xerxes believed it. He even sent thanks, and once more Sicinnus got away; perhaps, this time, with a tip.

Themistocles had his reasons. He knew himself: a patriot at need, but a racketeer not very long after. Sometime he might get caught at some shady business, and be exiled from Athens as he himself had exiled poor, honest Aristides. It might be just as well to have somewhere else to go.

For all his faults, he had two great virtues; they were loyalty and gratitude. When Sicinnus got back, he not only freed him from his slavery but set him up with land of his own and funds to run it, and made him a wealthy man.

The end of Themistocles' story happened much later; but I will tell it now. What he had feared came true; he was sent into exile. He went straight to Xerxes' court, reminded the King of his good services during the war, and asked for hospitality. Again the King believed him. He gave him a post at court, and he lived in Persia, honored and prosperous, for many years. But he had succeeded too well. Xerxes so trusted him that he asked him to command another army, and lead it against Greece. It was then the Athenian showed that under all his self-seeking trickery there was a bedrock of honor. Faced with the choice of betraying either his country or his kindly host, he found the one way left; he drank poison, and died.

But this was in the future. In the year of Salamis, the Persians fled to the north; and once again Æschylus tells the story in his play: how Xerxes led his forlorn men back towards the Hellespont, through the ruined lands where they had eaten up the harvest as they came down; half-starved, short even of water; meeting on the harsh mountain roads the cold winds of winter, the first falls of snow. Already the fast couriers had brought the news of defeat ahead; in Susa the people in the streets were wailing, tearing their clothes, and waiting in dread to hear the names of the fallen; while the Greeks of Ionia remembered how Xerxes had scourged the Hellespont, as if he were a god.

Even now the war was not quite over. Mardonius the Persian general, seeing his master sick at heart and wanting only to get home, asked for a fresh army and promised to turn defeat into victory. Xerxes agreed; from the vast manpower of the Empire another force was built, and crossed to Greece. Once more the Spartans squatted behind their Isthmus wall, and Athens stood alone. Once more the people fled, and Salamis was full of refugees. But this time, Mardonius had learned a lesson. Before trying more battles with this dangerous little city, he offered to spare it and give generous peace terms, if Athens would ally with Persia against Sparta and the rest.

The envoy he sent was Alexander of Macedon. He had done as little harm to the Greeks as he could while he followed Xerxes; his troops had done mostly garrison work in conquered towns; there was no reason why, in Athens, he should be greatly hated. And he himself advised the Athenians, quite sincerely, to accept the Persian terms. He would have grieved to see them destroyed; and after all he was not a democrat, but in his own kingdom an absolute ruler himself.

But this was the answer the Athenians made him: "We know the Persian strength is many times our own; you have no need to tell us. But our love of freedom is greater still. Say, therefore, to Mardonius, that while the sun still keeps his course across the sky, we will never make peace with Xerxes. No; we will stand against him, putting our trust in our gods whose shrines he burned. So tell him; and never bring this offer to us again. You are our guest and friend, and we would not like to harm you."

Then Mardonius laid Attica and Athens waste, destroying anything that had been left before. But the Spartans behind their wall heard of the Persian offer; and anxiety ate them up. If the Athenians, too, thought only of themselves, they might make peace yet. With their great navy added to the Persian strength, it would be the end for Sparta; their coasts could be invaded anywhere. At last they saw the folly of the wall, and agreed to help. They put their army in the field; and when the last battle was fought at Platæa on the Theban plain, Athenians and Spartans stood side by side.

In the dark of the night, before the battle, when neither side knew what the enemy would do, a horseman rode up in the night to the Greek camp. He would not give his name, but named the generals, and asked to speak with them. The sentries fetched them, for this did not look like a common man. When they came, the rider said to them, "The Persians have delayed so long because they cannot get good omens when they sacrifice. Now they have ceased to try; they will attack at daybreak, so be ready. If you win the battle, do something for my kingdom; and do not betray me to Xerxes, for it would be my death. I am Alexander of Macedon."

When he had spoken, he rode back to the Persian lines, and took up the station Mardonius had given him.

So the Greeks were ready, and won a decisive victory. Among the heaps of the fallen was Mardonius. The Spartan King Pausanias, when it was over, was looking at the slain, when someone said to him, "Now is your chance to treat the body of this Persian prince as Xerxes did the corpse of Leonidas, your kinsman." Perhaps the man hoped this would win him favor. But the Spartan said in scorn, "Has Leonidas not been avenged? And do you think I would better my good name by doing a barbarous thing no Greek would stoop to? I would rather be known for reverence and decency. Get out, and be thankful you go with a whole skin."

Mardonius' tent still stood, with all its splendors; it was the one Xerxes had brought to Greece to use himself. Pausanias, calling the cooks, bade them prepare a banquet, as if it were for Mardonius or the King; then he fetched his own army cooks to make a Spartan dinner, black bean-broth, cheese and barley bread. He had the two meals set side by side, and said laughing to the others, "Look! This is what Xerxes could get at home. Yet the fool came here, to rob us of our poverty."

Now it was time to burn thank-offerings upon the altars of the gods. But all the sacred fires in the shrines and temples had been put by the Persians to common uses. This was a pollution; the soothsayer said they must all be quenched, and rekindled only with sacred fire from Apollo's great altar at Delphi. It was more than forty miles off, and much of it over mountains. A Platæan soldier, a famous runner, whose name was Euchidas, offered to fetch the fire, saying he would be quicker than any other man. Though he had already fought a battle, he ran all the way there; he stopped only to take a ritual bath, so as to come pure before the god; then he ran back. Before sunset of that day he reached Platæa. He greeted his comrades, and gave them his burning torch; then his heart gave out, and he fell dead upon the field.

This was the final victory—a victory, said the Greeks, over the barbarians. "Barbarian" is a word they coined by mimicking foreign speech, *bar-bar*. It did not mean, as it does now, an untamed savage; yet it was an angry word, for people who destroy. The Persians were highly civilized, as a historian, or an archaeologist, would use the word. They had good order at home, efficient administration, and handsome cities; their jewelers and painters and sculptors made beautiful things. But if they had conquered Greece, they would have killed at the root almost all we value today, because they were not free.

All the best we know comes from the freedom of men to think: to think what is right to do, or what is true; to think why these things are so, and bring people round to one's view with reason, not with force. The Greek philosophers invented logic, by which false argument can be told from true. All this, when the Persians came, was springing up like a sapling, which will top the forest if left to grow, but if cut will quickly die. It lived, and our own tree springs from it.

All justice is logic, argued out in public, good evidence against bad. All science is logic about material things. And the honor of all professions is the honor of free men. The judge of a free people can judge upon the evidence, without threat or bribery; the doctor can keep the oath that came down from Greek Hippocrates, to put the good of his patient first in everything, never to betray his trust. The teacher cannot be made to teach a lie which suits someone in power. When these things crumble, civilization is dead within, even though all the people eat off gold.

The Athenians understood all this; the Spartans turned their backs on it. In less than a hundred years from Salamis, their fear and jealousy of the Athenian way would smoulder into war. But before that long bitter struggle bled the strength from Greece, she lived through the brilliant morning and noontime of her art and thought; no one could walk into that light, even her conquerors, and not be changed. Alexander the Great, the conqueror of the world, carried Greek thought as far to the east as India; and the Romans as far west as Britain.

This great upspringing of human genius gained strength from the past danger. When one takes on risk and hardship, one thinks out why. The Greeks came out of it thinking what they were and lived by; what a man ought to be, and what makes his life worth living; what he owes to God, his country, and other men.

In their temples and their statues, even in the little pictures painted on vases and jars, they showed the gods like men made perfect, and men in the image of the gods; not showing what they are in failure or in weakness, but what they should strive to be. They were not trying to escape the facts of life, but to work on life as the carver does on marble, and change the facts themselves. They thought that by loving beauty people would become more beautiful; that by hearing courage and wisdom praised, they would absorb courage and wisdom as plants draw in light and rain. And who shall say they were wrong?

When Athens was at the peak of greatness, a generation after the Persian wars, this was what Pericles the statesman said about the life they led there:

"Our form of government does not compete with others'; we do not imitate, we set the standard. We are called a democracy, because our state is run by the people, not the few. But while our law gives justice to all alike, the outstanding man is honored also. There are no closed circles in our public life; and in our private dealings we are not suspicious of each other. We do not take offense at our neighbor for living in the way he likes, nor give him the sour looks which punish though they break no bones. We are carefree in private, but responsible in public business; we are kept from doing evil by respect for authority and law, especially where it protects the man who is wronged.

"We have not forgotten how to relax; we have games and sacred feasts all through the year; our life at home is graceful, and our delight in these things keeps sadness from us. The fruits of the whole earth flow in to us, because of the greatness of our city.

"Athens is open to the world. We are not afraid of foreigners learning anything to use against us. Our trust is not in secret trickery, but in our own hearts and minds. The Spartans from their first youth are going through pain and labor to make them brave. We live at ease; yet we face danger as well as they. If we would sooner meet it light of heart, with courage built by habit, not enforced by law, are we not the gainers? For we love the beautiful, yet our tastes are simple; we cultivate our minds, yet keep our manliness. Those men are surely the bravest who, feeling most keenly the pains and pleasures of life, do not fear to risk it. In truth we shall not lack witnesses. What our greatness built will make us the wonder of this and every age hereafter."

So said Pericles. And if you go to Athens, you will find it true.

HISTORICAL NOTE

Nearly all we know about the Persian wars comes from the *History* of Herodotus. He lived and wrote in the latter half of the fifth century B.C., when a great many people who had been eyewitnesses of the events were still alive, and many more had heard about them at first hand. Herodotus was very careful to weigh the value of evidence; if he is only repeating hearsay, he always says so.

One great idea underlies all his book: that history is about *people*. He thought that character is destiny. He never writes about human beings as if they were economic units, statistics, or lines on a graph. He is full of stories which show what men are made of and how they behave in the great crises of their lives. This makes him the most interesting of all historians. His people are alive for us after two and a half thousand years. He was a great traveler. In spite of the hardships and dangers of travel in those times, he visited nearly all the places he wrote about, questioned witnesses himself, and looked over the battle-fields. If you want to see how Herodotus wrote, turn to page 106 and read on from "Till now the Greeks had been concerned to hold the pass" to the foot of the page. This passage is taken from his *History* almost word for word.

Plutarch, to whom we owe a great deal too, wrote very much later, mainly in the first century A.D. He was a Greek, at the time when world power had passed to Rome, but he spoke both Greek and Latin and was at home in either country. The value of his books is that the libraries he used owned important works of history which disappeared in the Dark Ages later. He did not write continuous history, like Herodotus, but he used a great deal of this precious material in his biographies of famous Greeks and Romans.

Rome was the center of the world; if he had stayed there, he could have been fashionable and rich. But he grew tired of its noise, its vicious competition and vulgar pleasures, and went back to Greece to live in quiet among his books. He was a follower of Apollo, the god of poets and writers; he became a priest of the oracle at Delphi and served there for many years—no doubt he used the temple records in his work. He never became a Christian, but the virtues he valued in his heroes ring just as true today. So vividly drawn are the people in his *Lives*, that writers in every age, from Shakespeare downward, have been inspired by reading them.

We have only one writer on the war who actually took part in it. This was the poet Æschylus, who certainly fought at Marathon (his brother was killed there) and probably at Artemisium, Salamis, and Platæa too. We cannot learn much history from him; he used only what he needed for his play, *The Persians,* but it brings the spirit of those times very near to us, and the sense of destiny the Athenians felt when their task was done. When he died, he had become a famous writer. But this was what he asked to have carved upon his tomb:

Under this monument lies
　Æschylus the Athenian,
Euphorion's son, who died
　in the wheatlands of Gela. The grove
of Marathon with its glories
　can speak of his valor in battle.
The long-haired Persian remembers
　and can speak of it too.

DATES OF THE CHIEF EVENTS

11th century B.C.	Dorians invade Greece from the north and seize lands in the Peloponnese, founding Sparta.
	Athenians and other Greeks found colonies in Asia Minor.
8th and 7th centuries B.C.	Rise of democracies, constitutional kings, oligarchies, and tyrannies.
546 B.C.	Cyrus of Persia defeats King Crœsus.
529 B.C.	Death of Cyrus. Cambyses succeeds to throne.
525 B.C.	Cambyses conquers Egypt.
521 B.C.	Death of Cambyses. Darius succeeds.
510 B.C.	Hippias the tyrant expelled from Athens.
499 B.C.	Ionians revolt with the help of Athenians. Sardis burned.

494 B.C.	Persians defeat Ionian fleet at Ladé. Darius plans revenge on Athens.
490 B.C.	First invasion of Greece. Persian fleet sails through the Cyclades to Marathon.
	Pheidippides runs to Sparta.
	Battle of Marathon. Athenian victory.
489 B.C.	Themistocles in power at Athens. He banishes Aristides.
485 B.C.	Death of Darius. Xerxes succeeds.
485–481 B.C.	Xerxes prepares his army.
480 B.C.	Second invasion of Greece. (August) Battle of Thermopylæ. (September) Battle of Salamis. Xerxes retires.
479 B.C.	Campaign of Mardonius. Battle of Platæa.
	Final victory of the Greeks.

GLOSSARY

ACROPOLIS: In Greek, "high point of the city." The acropolis of a Greek city-state such as Argos, Thebes, Athens, or Corinth was its strongest defense point—a walled fortress, built on high ground. The Acropolis of Athens is 260 feet high, 500 feet wide, and 1,150 feet long. During the Age of Pericles (463–429 B.C.) it was adorned with superb sculpture and architecture—including the famous Parthenon.

ARCHON: An Athenian officer of state, elected annually. Originally there were three archons: the *archon eponymos,* who was the chief officer of state; the *archon basilios,* who officiated primarily in connection with the sacred rites; and the *archon polymarchos,* who was the military leader. Eventually, six more archons, junior officers called *thesmothetai,* were added; these men were in charge of the law courts. At the time of the Persian Wars, the archons were elected. Later (circa 487 B.C.) they were chosen by lot.

CARNEAN FEAST: Sparta's most important religious event; a Doric festival in honor of Apollo, held each year in late summer. A race was run in which a youth was pursued by five others (if he was overtaken, good fortune for the city was assured for the year to come; if not, the reverse); and a feast was held in bowers resembling military tents. During the month of the Carnea no important undertakings could be begun.

CODRUS: The last king of ancient Athens. According to legend, it was prophesied at the time of the Dorian invasion (eleventh century B.C.) that Athens could be saved only if the king of Athens were slain by the enemy. Therefore King Codrus voluntarily went to the Dorian camp—in disguise, for the Dorians knew of the Athenian prophecy and would not have wished to fulfill it. He provoked an argument and allowed himself to be killed. When the Dorians learned whom they had slain, they stopped all further attempts to conquer Athens.

CRESSETS: Iron vessels of oil, or metal baskets containing wood, suspended as lanterns or mounted as flambeaux.

DELPHI: In ancient Greece, people sought advice in the form of oracles—prophecies made by gods in answer to human questions. The spirit of the god was supposed to enter the body of the priestess, who then answered suppliants' questions, sometimes in delirium produced by religious ecstasy aided by drugs, sometimes in the voice of the god. A priest was at hand to interpret the prophecy in case the prophetess was rambling or incoherent; a second priest turned the interpretation into verse. Some of the prophecies recorded show a genuine gift of second sight. In other cases it is evident that the priests formulated an ambiguous answer to avoid the risk of a false prediction.

The word *oracle* is used not only of the actual message, but of the prophetic shrine and the priestess who spoke for the god.

There were many oracles in ancient Greece; some of the most famous were the oracle of Zeus at Dodona (where the god's messages were interpreted from the rustling of a sacred oak and the sound of its birds) and the oracles of Apollo at Klaros and Branchidai. But the most influential oracle was at Delphi, upon a high shelf of Mount Parnassus. In exchange for answers to their questions, suppliants left costly gifts at Delphi. City-states such as Athens, Sparta, Thebes, and Corinth had constructed special treasuries there to house their gifts to the god.

Before Apollo took charge of the shrine, after his victory over the serpent Pytho, it had belonged to the ancient Earth Goddess of many names: Gæa, Rhea, and latterly Demeter (see ELEUSIS). The title of the prophetess, the Pythia, was taken from the name of the serpent and shows that the cult was older than that of Apollo. The sacred games, held in the god's honor near Delphi every four years (a year before the Olympic contests), were called the Pythian Games.

The Navel Stone at Delphi, which was kept in the oracular cave bound in a sacred woolen net, was believed by the Greeks to mark the center of the earth. According to legend, this very stone had saved the life of Zeus in his infancy. His father, Kronos, having received a prophecy that one of his sons would overthrow him, devoured them one by one. When Zeus was born his mother, Rhea, gave Kronos a stone to swallow instead, and brought up Zeus in secret to fulfill the prophecy. He overthrew Kronos's barbaric rule and fathered the race of the young Olympians—Apollo, Artemis, Dionysos, Hermes, Ares, Athene. Some of the other

Olympians, however, were descended from the ancient line of Kronos: Hera and her son Hephæstus, Poseidon, Demeter, and the ageless love goddess, Aphrodite.

DEMETER THE MOTHER: *see* ELEUSIS.

ELEUSIS: An ancient city of Attica, twelve miles northwest of Athens. It was the site of a large temple of Demeter, the Great Mother, wherein were held highly secret religious ceremonies that are believed to have had their origin in fertility ceremonies of the ancient religions of Greece before the advent of the Olympian gods. The purpose of these ceremonies, known as the Mysteries, was to achieve a mystical union between worshipers and deities such as Demeter, Dionysos, and Persephone. In ancient times, counterparts of the Greek Demeter could be found all over the world—Cybele in Persia, Isis in Egypt, Astarte among the Phœnicians, and Ishtar in Babylonia and Assyria.

EPHORS, COUNCIL OF: An executive, legislative, and judicial board of five Spartan citizens, selected annually, usually by the drawing of lots. Although the Spartan kings, two of whom reigned at a time, were recognized as the only authorized military commanders, the ephors had full discretion in recruiting troops. They could also bring a king to trial for alleged military errors.

EUCHIDAS: The death of this runner after the battle of Platæa is often mistakenly ascribed to Pheidippides after Marathon. History has no record of how, or when, Pheidippides died.

THE GREAT MOTHER: *see* ELEUSIS.

HALICARNASSUS: An ancient city of Caria, a province of the Persian empire. It was the birthplace of Herodotus, as well as the site of the great tomb of King Mausolus—one of the Seven Wonders of the World.

HELLAS: Greece. The name is derived from Hellen, the legendary ancestor of all Greek peoples (Hellenes), including the Dorians. Hellen was the son of Prometheus, the Titan who angered Zeus by bringing fire and the arts to mankind.

HELLENE: *see* HELLAS.

HOUSE SNAKE: The sacred serpent that lived in a cave under the Acropolis of Athens was believed to be the final earthly form of Erechtheus, a legendary Athenian king reputed to have established the Panathenæa and to have invented the four-wheeled chariot. His father was said to be Hephæstus (Vulcan), the god of fire and metalwork, and his mother was Gæa, the earth-goddess later known under the names Rhea and Demeter.

From the most ancient times, sacred snakes were thought to embody the guardian spirits of a building. They were connected with the powers of earth, and if they made their holes under the foundations their presence was protective. In Crete special jars were put down to hold their food, with holes for them to enter. Earth tremors are frequent all over Greece; it is likely that, in common with many other wild creatures, these snakes would sense a coming earthquake, and leave a threatened house. Their departure would then come to be remembered as an omen of future evil.

HYMETTUS: A mountain range extending from northeast of Athens southward to the Saronic Gulf. It has been celebrated since ancient times for its honey.

ISTHMIAN GAMES: Games held near Corinth in honor of Poseidon, god of the sea, in the spring of the first and third years of the four-year Olympic cycle (see OLYMPIC GAMES). Like the Olympic Games, they were attended by people from all of Greece.

LACONIA: The country of the Spartans.

LIBATION: The pouring of wine as a sacrifice to a god.

MAGI (*singular* MAGUS): A priestly caste of ancient Persia, probably originating among the Medes before the conquest by Cyrus (see MEDES). Almost nothing is known of their religious beliefs. They were greatly revered for their wisdom, particularly in the interpretation of dreams and in the warding-off of demons.

MEDES: An ancient people of northwest Iran, whose empire was conquered by Cyrus of Persia circa 550 B.C. The Medes were held in honor by their conquerors. The Persians adopted the ceremonial of the Median court, and many Medes were employed as satraps and generals.

MOUNT PARNASSUS: *see* DELPHI.

MYSTERIES: *see* ELEUSIS.

MYCENÆ: A city-state in the Peloponnese. At the time of the Persian Wars, it was a minor power that still used the half-ruined fortifications of King Agamemnon, who had ruled Mycanæ in its long-past days of greatness. Agamemnon commanded the Greek armies against Troy. On his return from the war, his wife, Clytemnestra, murdered him. Then, to avenge the crime, Clytemnestra's son, Orestes, murdered her. This story of the curse of the House of Atreus is told in a trilogy of plays by Æschylus: *Agamemnon, The Choëphoræ,* and *The Eumenides.*

NISÆA: A region in Media (perhaps near the Caspian Gates) famous for its breed of horses.

OLYMPIA: A small plain in the land of Elis in Greece. It was a center of the worship of Zeus, and the great temple of Olympian Zeus was built here. Here on the plain in Elis—not at the foot of Mount Olympus in Pieria—the Olympic Games were initiated in 776 B.C. and held every four years for many centuries thereafter. The initiation of the Olympic Games marked the point from which the ancient Greeks dated their calendar, the way the birth of Christ marks the beginning of the Christian calendar. The four-year cycle between the Games was called an Olympiad. Athletes from all the Hellenic states participated in the Games, and a sacred truce was declared between participants and spectators from any nations that might then be at war with each other.

OLYMPIAD: *see* OLYMPIA.

OLYMPIC GAMES: *see* OLYMPIA.

ORACLE: *see* DELPHI.

ORMUZ (*or* AHURAMAZDA): The supreme deity of the ancient Persian religion. Ormuz—the god of light and goodness, the creator of the world, and guardian of mankind—was believed to be involved in a constant struggle with Ahriman, the spirit of evil and darkness.

PROPHET *or* PROPHETESS: A person who can foretell the future—either in the manner of the Pythia at Delphi (see DELPHI) or in the manner of a soothsayer (see SOOTHSAYER).

PANATHENÆA: The great festival of Athene, patron goddess of Athens. Every spring the women of Athens embroidered a beautiful and costly robe for the statue of the goddess seated in the temple of Athene on the Acropolis. The procession in which flower-decked maidens carried this robe to the Acropolis was the climax of the festival.

PANATHENAIC GAMES: The games that were held during the annual Festival of Athene (the PANATHENÆA). Athletes from all Attica participated.

PAPYRUS: A tufted marsh plant, the solid stem of which was used in ancient Egypt as fuel, as food, in the making of paper, and in the making of twine, mats, and cloth.

PYTHIA: *see* DELPHI.

SATRAP: A governor of a province within the Persian Empire.

THE SIGHT: A soothsayer's "second sight," or his ability to interpret omens and foretell the future.

SOOTHSAYER-PRIEST: The soothsayer-priest predicted the future by studying physical omens, which occurred either in nature or in ceremonial procedures—such as killing a kid and studying its entrails. Unlike the priest or priestess of an oracle, he did not speak the messages of a god.

SUNIUM HEAD: A rocky promontory on the coast of the Ægean Sea, southeast of Athens. It is the site of a temple to Poseidon.

TRIREME: An ancient war galley, propelled by three banks of oars.

INDEX

[Figures in **boldface** indicate pages upon which illustrations appear.]

Format by Morris Karol
Set in Linotype Baskerville
Composed by American Book–Stratford Press
Printed by Murray Printing Co.
Bound by American Book–Stratford Press
HARPER & ROW, PUBLISHERS, INCORPORATED